INJICHAAG

INJICHAAG

My Soul in Story

Anishinaabe Poetics
in Art and Words

RENE MESHAKE
WITH KIM ANDERSON

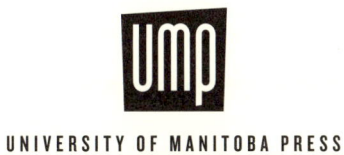

UNIVERSITY OF MANITOBA PRESS

Injichaag: My Soul in Story
Anishinaabe Poetics in Art and Words
© Rene Meshake 2019
Introduction and Epilogue © Kim Anderson 2019

23 22 21 20 19   1 2 3 4 5

University of Manitoba Press
Winnipeg, Manitoba, Canada
Treaty 1 Territory
uofmpress.ca

Cataloguing data available from Library and Archives Canada
ISBN 978-0-88755-848-1 (PAPER)
ISBN 978-0-88755-850-4 (PDF)
ISBN 978-0-88755-849-8 (EPUB)

Cover design: Kirk Warren
Cover photo: Joan Bruder
Interior design: Jess Koroscil

Printed in Canada

The poem "Still Here" and the story "Andjiiana Gitodem" were first accepted for publication in *The Other Side of 150*, a volume of essays slated to appear in 2020 through Wilfrid Laurier University Press.

This book has been published with the help of a grant from the Federation for the Humanities and Social Sciences, through the Awards to Scholarly Publications Program, using funds provided by the Social Sciences and Humanities Research Council of Canada.

The University of Manitoba Press acknowledges the financial support for its publication program provided by the Government of Canada through the Canada Book Fund, the Canada Council for the Arts, the Manitoba Department of Sport, Culture, and Heritage, the Manitoba Arts Council, and the Manitoba Book Publishing Tax Credit.

Funded by the Government of Canada | Canadä

*Dedicated to my dear wife Joan and my son Aaron
in whom I am well blessed*

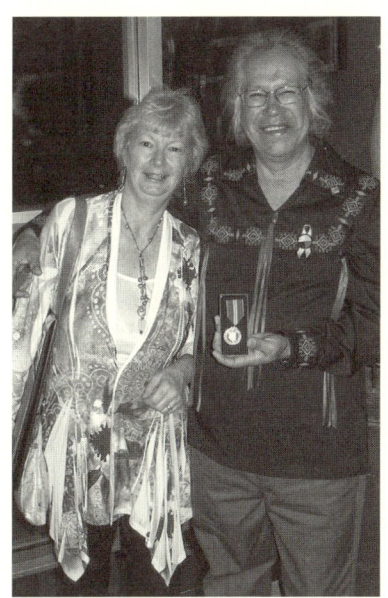
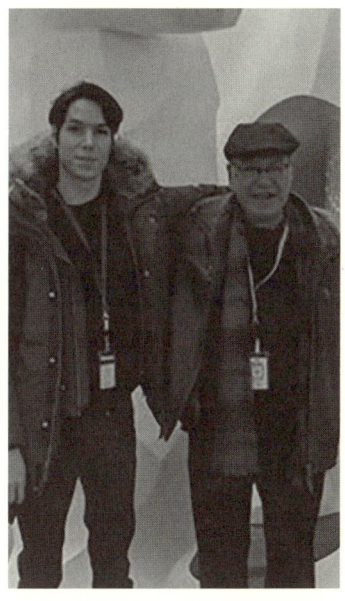

Contents

PART TWO: NIBINAABE — STORIES OF WARNING

PART THREE: WIKWEDONG — STORIES OF LOSS

PART FOUR: BIMISI — STORIES OF PROTECTION
AND TRANSITION

PART SIX: PAPAWANGANI — STORIES OF
HEALING THROUGH ART

PART SEVEN: MIGISIWIGANJ — STORIES
OF REGENERATION

Andotamowin: Invocation

After I settled on **Injichaag** *as the title of my book, I noticed the similarity between inji[chaa]g and ru[ach]. Ruach is the word for soul or spirit in Hebrew. Injichaag means "my soul" in Anishinaabemowin. It is in my soul that I have the power to choose, to desire, and to be angry. I've chosen to write my story.*

A copy of my family tree lit up in my hands. Old records, dating back to 1834. Records that told of dozens of traditional Anishinaabemowin names. Names that I had never heard and knew nothing about. Now, before my eyes, I could see how many of my Anishinaabe ancestors had a single, distinct, given name. No first or last names. No first and last!

It's been a long, long time. 1834. And now, my quest for your given names, mishomisak (ancestors)! Enclosed by your Anishinaabe names and birthrights, I would have transformed into manhood, a named one, like all of you.

Nookomis! Grandmother. Gitchi-Aya'aa. The records show that your maiden name was Megan or Megwan, a feather. It was also Kitchi'gabwik. Kitchi (great); gabaw (to stand fast); wik (woman). A distinct description of your character and a way of approaching life; for once you decided on a course of action, nothing could deter you. Your name personifies determination; your title predestined the person you would grow up to be. Falling down; each time you got up, you grew stronger.

Nookomis, you met Shibagabaw. Shiba (underneath); gabaw (to stand); aw (the one). He was the one to stand underneath, to provide and protect you. He was the inini (man), and the root word there is nindj (hand). One hand to provide, the other to protect. You were the iskwew (woman), and the word is taken from ishkode (fire). Fire symbolizes life, and you were the life giver. Inini then tends the fire. Gender balance, partners, harmony, equality.

I honour your generation, Nookomis Kitchi'gabwik! I roll back the birchbark years to see your glory and knowledge, wisdom and vision. It's been a long, long time.

I remember your brother, Menawegishig. Me (he whose); nawe (good voice); gishig (sky). He gave your skies good voice, all his life. I benefit from his prayers still today. I remember how much trouble he had walking. He'd slowly unpack his hunting rifle, a .30-30 Winchester, ornate and polished, whispering blessings, moose prayers. He was going moose hunting in the evening. One last push of the cleaning rod into the rifle bore, and off we went, bent with anticipation. We knew. It was as if the moose was waiting for us, his muscles rippling in the dusk as he dipped his head in the water. One last dip, and Menawegishig aimed, fired, and the moose gave his life to us. Menawegishig, as was his custom, divided the meat, and gave each family their helping. Although he was disabled, he provided like any hunter of his generation. He was Menawegishig!

I'll never forget your sister, Wemboma. Wem (she whose); boma (voice wakens). She was there with us at the hunt. She, Wemboma, wakened Menawegishig's prayers so that the moose could be prepared. She had lived many winters. Bibooniwesi. Biboon (winter); iwesi (way of life). Her smile and her deeper tan of springtime proclaimed renewal. She was laughter.

I can still hear your laughter, Wemboma. You always had a tin of snuff or chewing tobacco by your side. There abides my memory! The culture of traditional names has been still, silent, but your voice has awakened me.

Our names have been silenced since 1921, when names like John, Michel, Theresa, Sam, Sarah, David, Mary, Elizabeth, and Peter emerged among my own Shebagabow family. A change was coming to our home-land with the changing of names, a changing of titles and then interrupted promise. Our ancestors had a word that spoke to that promise: nakoda-mowin. You would nakodam (consent) to what the grandmothers asked you to do for the community. You were appreciated, nookomisak, the grandmothers knew your deep, inner desire for a secure community.

I never knew all my Shebagabow uncles and aunts. Some left too early to give me cousins. But they had promise, potential, and they consented, even with their interrupted lives.

John Shebagabow, I never hugged you. In your short life, you were an Anishinaabe with a Hebrew name. John. Meaning the grace of the Lord. Uncle John, if I were there, if I had the honour, I would name you Zhawendji gogishig, Mercy from the Sky. A mediator. A diplomat. A partner.

Wherever you wander on earth, the sky reminds you to respect the confidences of your Anishinaabeg nation.

And Michel, a Hebrew name denoting a gift from God. In French, it's "for he who is like God." Michel, you were excited by the changes in our community; the strange traditions of ringing church bells. The pace of your soul was moved by a sense of adventure. A visionary. A friend of freedom. Uncle Michel, if I were there, if I had the honour, I would name you Pagidini gishig. Gift from the First Sky. Adventurer. But your short life crushed your desires. The pace of your community expired, and with it your promise.

And Theresa, an Anishinaabekwe with a Greek name, meaning "to harvest." A reaper. An inspiration. Even when you were too young, you gathered ideas on spiritual matters. But you were not given a life of service. Dedication died. Truth and justice cried. Aunt Theresa, if I were there, if I had the honour, I would name you Mamaa winok. Harvest Woman Leader. Dedicated one. But your desires were buried with you.

And Sam. Anishinaabe born with a Hebrew name that means "sun child." A bright sun of independence rose. But before you reached the age of Ogimakan, you left this world. Harmony left with you. Uncle Sam, if I were there, if I had the honour, I would name you Saagate wishkang. Sun Coming Out of the Clouds Walker. Wherever you walked, you would restore harmony from the imbalances brought on by the dark disrupting clouds. Where are the original beautiful things now that you're gone?

And Sarah, a princess in the Hebrew language. Like your brothers, you respected the confidences of your people. But aristocracy did not exist in the homeland; no princess, no royalty, no hierarchy to be found in your Anishinaabe community. Diplomacy was everyone's job. Then, life cut you down too soon, before anyone knew what a princess was. Aunt Sarah, if I were there, if I had the honour, I would name you Widjindino waabanok. Companion of the Dawn. Your brief appearance on earth taught your people the meaning of companionship.

And David, beloved or friend in the Hebrew language. Born in the Anishinaabe culture, where the ability to lead was highly valued. A leader. A trailblazer. A frontrunner. You were to be a positive force in all the lives that you might have touched. Uncle David, if I were there, if I had the honour, I would name you Wiidji kiwe wishkang. He Who Walks Friendship to Life. I feel your spirit. I felt loved, even though you were born in 1918, so long ago.

And Mary, which means "wished for child" in Hebrew. A minidimoie—(matriarch)—wished for child. You were going to be trained to be Ogima (leader). Chief. Minidmoieg recognized your personal independence at an early age. Instead, you tasted death. Aunt Mary, if I were there, if I had the honour, I would name you Dawen dagoso wiik. Desired Woman. Dawendagosowiik, the desire of the Anishinaabeg nation. Instead, you tasted death, and bitterness began.

And Peter, I remember you. Your name Peter is a biblical one meaning "a rock" or "stone." You were a leader, and a powerful personality for me. You taught me to defer to my Nookomis (grandmother), as I saw you do it. This tradition, this politeness, always extended to the Okomissaag—grandmothers of the community. Although I was orphaned, you gave me Shebagabows, cousins of stone. Uncle Peter, if I were there, if I had the honour, I would name you Assini kawi dang. Man Who Speaks Stones to Life. This name, my late uncle! Give me courage, determination to finish my lifetime anikanotawing work.

And then there was Elizabeth, my mother, with a Hebrew name too. Elizabeth means my Creator is bountiful, my Creator is plenty. A teacher. A mystic, until tuberculosis took her away. My tongue was cut out and I never said Mom no more. Elizabeth, mom, if I were there, if I had the honour, I would name you Kisha disi winok. A Woman

Who Walks Benevolence to Life. I only met you once, and once was enough to walk me into life. I learn, I teach.

Mom, you lived just long enough to name me, Rene Andre, renewed manly in the French language. I grew up to be an Anishinaabe man with a French name. What is my Anishinaabe name? Mom!

Enclosed by our Anishinaabe names, my birthright, it would have transformed me.

I am known today as Rene Meshake from my paternal grandfather. But originally his odishinikasowin name was Mishakigishig. Misha (hover over and descend); aki (earth); gishig (sky). At birth, in the vision quest of his name, an Elder saw a damselfly, metallic green, long and lean, hovering, descending over the waters and among the reeds. Mishoomis, you were mishakigishig, your role, and a way to carry yourself as you journeyed through the odena, the heart of your community. You earned respect. "They" anglicized your name to Meshake; you did not change in form or character.

As I research the sound, cadence, imagery, and meaning of my family's traditional and Anishinaabe ancestral names I feel sad. I feel deprived. I feel robbed. But in the Gichi-Manido/Creator's world there is no accident, luck, or randomness. There is a purpose to everything, even to naming a child, even to the Hebrew names my aunts and uncles were given. Perhaps those names are prophetic; perhaps their names have not happened yet. They prophesized something glorious, something new about our Anishinaabeg arts and culture.

We will return to our names. Names embedded in our homelands. True mishina wewi win (sharing). Call it mystical. Call it whimsical. Quixotic even. But I see signs. I see symbols. I see meanings.

There is a will, embedded in our homelands.

And in the act of mishinawew, you share. You songa'ona. Songa (strengthen); ona (the other). Mishomisak, ancestors!

The Anishinaabe word for Invocation would be Andotamowin (to ask, to petition, to request, to appeal). Andotamowin also means that you are still and listening for your answer after you've invoked for help or prayed.

INJICHAAG

Introduction

KIM ANDERSON

I first met Rene Meshake after we spotted each other at a "schmooze-fest" networking arts event in the city of Guelph in 1997, not long after we had both moved there with our young families. As two Indigenous individuals living in a small southwestern Ontario city, we gravitated toward each other. Rene recalls I told him, "I'm a writer" and he replied, "I'm an artist." As for the rest, he says, "I don't remember what else we talked about—I guess we were 'schmoozing!'" That was the first of many conversations in our evolving twenty-year friendship.

Over those years, I have frequently been audience to Rene's storytelling, both in public venues as well as through the oral history sessions we have done for various projects. What has always captured me about Rene's life story—a familiar one of colonization and recovery—is that he frames it in such a unique way: through the life of an artist and the lens of a poet. It seemed to me that Rene's telling begged for a memoir and so, about seven years ago, we agreed to work on it together.

Now that it's done, this book seems more than a memoir. Like other works of Indigenous literature, it defies easy categorization as it engages Anishinaabe philosophy, history, linguistics, literary theory, theology/spiritual knowledge—much of it wrapped up in a good dose of teachings from "Nookomis" (Rene's maternal grandmother). Now that it's done, *Injichaag* offers this knowledge through a collection of short pieces I see as gems, each one whole and shiny unto itself, but when strung together offering an entirely new, unique, and intricate expression of Anishinaabe life. The pieces in the book can thus be picked up and read at any point, but they also inform each other when read in the order they appear. Collectively, they express the *jichaagw*, the soul of the teller while also telling the larger story of the Anishinaabeg.

Perhaps this is the only way a memoir might have turned out for Rene Meshake, a multidisciplinary artist, with a practise so freely eclectic that it, too, defies categorization. Trained as a visual artist, Rene also works regularly as a performer and storyteller—and now that he is in his seventies, he works as a digital media "Techno Elder." Perhaps the scope of his approach and work is best exemplified in an email he sent me while I was writing this introduction:

Fri/6/1/2018, 3:42 pm
Bozho cheers! Niidji:
The manuscript is beginning to take on a life of its own.
It has a "slingshot effect" and you land in the most
pleasant places.
I mean that today, we drove to Oakville to buy 2 cedar Native
flutes in Em and F#.
The F# is a drone and now I find that I can travel beyond the
edge of the universe.

As liberated as this is, it is important to recognize that Rene's sovereign approach to art and living, grounded in Anishinaabe-gikendosowin (Ojibway knowledge) was carved out in spite of violent colonial attempts to oppress, constrain, and restrict his jichaagw (soul). As Rene explains in the story "Boxes, Circles, and Arcs," his early, spirited practise of creating art around the storytelling fires of his grandmother was smothered in Indian residential school. It was there that he temporarily lost expression through the restrictions they placed on his "pagan" artistic practise; a stifling that was exacerbated after he suffered sexual abuse at the hands of a school staff member. In *Injichaag*, Rene talks about how these colonial and oppressive practises "derailed a whole generation of us," but he always circles back to "*art, language, forgiveness,*" a fitting description of what is found in this book.

Injichaag tells Rene's life story thematically according to a series of paintings, which are matched with accompanying poems, stories, and word bundles. There is a logic to the sparse way the book unfolds, to what the spaces and silent places tell, and to how Rene interprets Anishinaabemowin words as bundles that tie the narrative together. Rene is passionate about working with his Anishinaabemowin dialect and in encouraging learners to develop new dialects by using living and diverse approaches, as he points out in "A Few Words about Anishinaabemowin, Dialects, and the Use of Language in this Book." As such, the Anishinaabemowin word bundles are not offered as direct translations of words—but as storied entities, taken apart and explored for the rich teachings and themes they carry for Rene.

Injichaag has an overall chronological flow, but periodically moves backward and forward in time to situate the material where it is best suited. The thematic sections offer stories involving the following:

Nurturing (Part I: Odinimanganikadjigan),
Warnings (Part II: Nibinaabe),
Loss (Part III: Wikwedong),
Protection and Transition (Part IV: Bimisi),
Recovery (Part V: Miskwadesshimo),
Healing through Art (Part VI: Papawangani), and
Regeneration (Part VII: Migisiwaganj).

We hope these themes resonate in the lives of Indigenous peoples across Turtle Island and beyond, as they touch on universal experiences in the human life course.

For those looking for more chronological and contextual information, I will briefly outline Rene's life course here, framed according to Anishinaabe life stage theory, and with epigraphs from Odawa Elder Liza Mosher.[1]

The Good Life (1948–c. 1958)

*"When the child is seven years old, they
should have all the foundations for a good life."*[2]

Rene was born in January 1948 at the hospital in Nakina, a railway
town located about sixty kilometres north of Geraldton in northwestern Ontario. His father's family lived nearby in Aroland, and
his mother was from Long Lake #58 First Nation, about forty-five
kilometres southeast. At the time of Rene's birth, reserve settlement
was relatively recent in the territory: Long Lake had become a reserve in 1914, following the 1850 Robinson Superior treaty nego-
tiations, and Aroland was a small settlement that wasn't recognized
as a reserve until 1985. Rene spent his first three years living with
his parents in Aroland, near the traditional hunting territories of his
paternal grandfather.

The area had a history of trapping and trading; many of the
Anishinaabeg in Aroland had lived on the shores of the Esnagami
Lake before creating a settlement in the early 1900s to engage in fur
trade activity with the regional Hudson's Bay Post.[3] Rene notes that
the Anishinaabeg first called the area Oongona gaming—translated as
"spring water lake portage," and that it was also a traditional gathering
place for families who had been trapping all winter. The Aroland population now includes former members of Long Lake #58, Ginoogaming,
Eabametoong, Marten Falls, and Fort William First Nations, but was
historically a mixed (Indian) status and non-status community, with
169 people recorded when the first statistics were taken in 1954.[4]

The fur trade dated back to the early 1700s, and in the late 1800s
forestry was introduced as a growing area of settler economic inter-
est. In 1933 the Arrow Land Logging Company opened a sawmill,
and Oongona gaming was renamed after the company that ran the
mill until 1941.[5] Mining came into the territory later with a "gold rush"
that started in 1934, followed by the opening of eight gold mines in
the region between 1936 and 1970.[6] During the Second World War
there was also a U.S.–operated radar base in the area.[7]

When the Arrow Land Logging Company decided to close in 1941, they burned the mill, leaving the population with piecemeal work and shattered hopes for health services that had started to develop in the 1930s.[8] In 1946, the Hudson's Bay Company also shut down activity in the area by closing their regional post. Rene points out that his people knew how to survive from what they harvested from the land, although as early as the 1930s there were reports of depleted game in the Ginoogaming area due to the clear-cutting of timber.[9] These problems were coupled with the fact that settler timber industries had not provided employment for local Indigenous peoples as they had promised.[10]

During this period, Nakina was a busy stop along the National Transcontinental (NT) Railway. The NT line had been built in 1913 to move grain east from Winnipeg to Quebec City, and in 1923 the Canadian National Railway (CNR) built a connecting line between Nakina and Longlac, increasing the significance of both as thriving service towns. The railway was thus a central feature in Rene's childhood; it was a source of employment and settlement for Native and non-Native people alike. By the 1940s northern trappers were setting up tents close to the railway for the purpose of visiting the stores and trading posts that had cropped up. Some built log cabins, moving back and forth between the railway and the traplines.[11] Stores and churches accommodated the railway crews and the mixed, non-status, and off-reserve communities on the route. The CNR tracks went through the traditional territory of Rene's maternal grandmother, and he remembers that some of her friends and relatives ended up marrying "lonely crewmen or section foremen who worked for the railway." The men in Rene's family also worked on the CNR, which, as Rene points out, provided "the only decent wage in those days," supplementing trapping and harvesting activities.

When Rene was three years old, both of his parents were sent to the Indian Hospital tuberculosis sanitarium in Fort William, ending his early years in Aroland. Rene's younger brother Kenny went to live with his father's side of the family, and Rene went to his "Nookomis," his maternal grandmother. As Rene would say, his grandmother then began his "bush university" education, as she lived a land-based life, moving from their odena (village) settlement in her traditional territory of Pagwashing, to her house on the reserve beside the church in Longlac, and back.

During his years with his grandmother, Rene periodically attended Indian day schools in Longlac and Aroland, but most of his learning came from time spent with her, off reserve and out on the land. Stories from this period demonstrate that the Anishinaabeg of Rene's childhood were operating from collectivist; Indigenous feminist; and environmentally, ethically, and spiritually sound principles and practises—all which come through in the word bundles that he shares in this book, which were taught to him by his grandmother. Life with "Nookomis" thus represents "the good life." As Rene has said, he is forever grateful for being gete ombigidj, "old lady raised."

The Fast Life (c. 1955–1966)

". . . everything starts coming at you fast."[12]

The good life of Rene's childhood came to an abrupt ending at the age of ten when he was sent to the McIntosh Indian Residential School in northwestern Ontario. With this act, Rene became one of the estimated 150,000 children who were interned in these schools from the time they opened in the late 1800s to when the last one closed in 1996.[13] In 1920, the *Indian Act*, the federal legislation governing "Indians and lands reserved for Indians" in Canada, was amended so the government could compel any "Indian" child to attend residential school. Children who ran away from residential schools faced arrest by Indian Affairs employees and constables.[14] By 1931 there were eighty schools in operation, and Rene entered the system around the time of its peak enrolment year (1956–57), about ten years before the federal government finally began to look into ways of shutting the schools down.[15]

As the Truth and Reconciliation Commission of Canada has documented, Indian residential schools were designed as tools of assimilation with the primary purpose of stripping Indigenous peoples

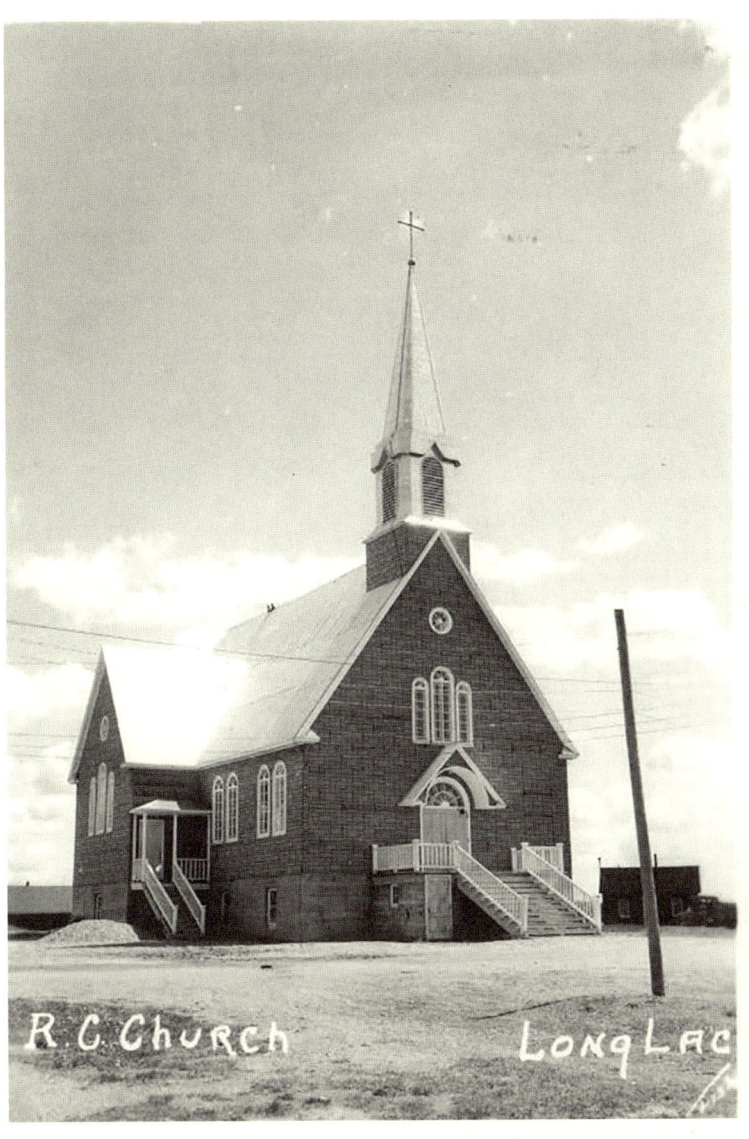

Church of the Infant Jesus, Longlac, Ontario, 1949–2018.

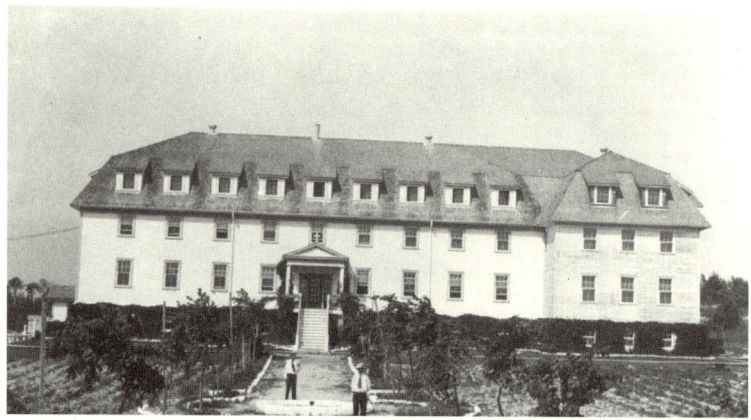

McIntosh Indian Residential School, 1927. Credit: Josias Fiddler, Virtual Museum of Canada.

of their lands, languages, and cultures.[16] Much of their daily routine involved doing chores to keep the schools running. What education the students did receive was minimal; training suited for creating labourers. These schools, funded by the federal government and run by Roman Catholic, Anglican, United, Methodist, and Presbyterian Churches, were also characterized by rampant and unchecked physical, mental, emotional, spiritual, and sexual abuse. They were, as John Milloy documented in his groundbreaking book on the subject, "a national crime."[17]

There is very little in *Injichaag* about Rene's time in residential school; those wishing to learn more on this subject will find it elsewhere in the robust body of testimony, scholarly, and autobiographical literature detailing residential school life.[18] Much of what is found in that literature aligns with Rene's experiences of abuse and the resulting feelings of shame and inferiority. In *Injichaag*, Rene only briefly touches on his experience at McIntosh with a poem about the sexual abuse he suffered at the hands of a lay brother. The poem "McIntosh" also depicts how liberating it was to hear about the school burning down in 1967. Although this is the only place where Rene describes life at residential school, the sexual abuse, involuntary confinement, denigration of his language and culture, and oppression of his artistic practise underpins a lot of the other material in the book. This is because the residential school years represented a breaking point from "the good life" Rene experienced with his grandmother and set the path for struggles he would face in the decades that followed.

While Rene was at McIntosh, both his mother and his Nookomis passed away, in 1960 and 1961 respectively, adding to his losses. He stayed in the system until he was sixteen, spending his final years at St. Margaret's Indian Residential School in Fort Frances where his brother Ken was also in attendance. From there he went on to high school at Westgate Collegiate in Thunder Bay. Rene reports feeling relieved to arrive in a mainstream school, as he wanted to disassociate from "Indians" at the time. In spite of these feelings of low self-worth and shame related to Indigeneity coming out of residential school, Rene made it through high school and managed to keep working on his art. The school recognized his talent and encouraged him to pursue post-secondary training. Looking for another escape, Rene left Thunder Bay at the age of eighteen to study graphic design at Sheridan College in Toronto.

Wandering and Wondering (c. 1966–1991)
*"The wandering life is when you wander all over,
looking for different answers and teachers."*[19]

It was 1966 when Rene took off for Sheridan, in pursuit, partly, of the hippies that he had heard of and who held appeal because they wore their hair long and their shirts untucked! In the story "Get an Education," Rene gives us a glimpse of life as an art school student in this era, which, as one might imagine, involved a lot of red wine, "grass," and engagement with the surreal. After graduating from Sheridan, Rene had several years of "wandering and wondering" drifting through multiple jobs, cities, and living arrangements. He first moved to Ottawa where his brother Ken was living and where he found work as a graphic artist. He wasn't able to shake the restlessness caused by residential school trauma, however, nor the yearning to be out on the land in his home territory. Before long he was back at home, working as a firefighter with his father. For the next decade or so, Rene worked in firefighting and tree planting, living on and off with his father, grandfather, and uncles in Geraldton. Although he was offered graphic design jobs with the Ministry of Natural Resources (MNR) and Kimberly Clark, he preferred to stick to outdoor work. In the story "Restless," he notes that being in the forest also helped him deal with the rage and depression he was fighting and which he was increasingly medicating with alcohol.

In the late '70s, Rene went back to Confederation College in Thunder Bay for retraining. He chose electronics, mostly because he was curious about how to build the radios that he had listened to as a youth on the logging roads in Aroland, swaggering to Elvis and Ricky Nelson. This training landed him a job wiring streetcars with Canada Car. He married in 1978, thinking that the stability of a wife, home, and stepchildren would help him with his progressive alcoholism. In spite of these efforts, things deteriorated, and around 1983 Rene left everything and made the decision to jump on a train bound for British Columbia. His plan was to find more forest firefighting work while enjoying a change of scene in the mountains. Rene never made it to British Columbia; when he got off the train in Winnipeg his first inclination was to admire the carvings in the old station, and his second was to find the liquor store.

Rene spent about three years in Winnipeg doing odd jobs, living in rooming houses and drinking, until he received news in 1986 that his father had died. This was the beginning of the darkest period of his life; almost six years of homelessness in Toronto.

Truth (c. 1991–1995)

"The fourth stage is truth life; it shows what your gifts and talents are."[20]

Rene tells his story of coming out of alcoholism and homelessness in the story "Eshpadinaa." This story makes the link between language, cultural revival, and survival, bundled into a teaching about the Anishinaabemowin origins of Toronto's Spadina Avenue. It was there, wandering through Chinatown one morning, that Rene found himself crying out "give me life or death!" He now celebrates that day, August 12, 1991, as the beginning of sobriety and healing.

Rene made it through with the help of the Native organizations that had been growing throughout the 1980s and '90s.[21] His path to truth by returning to his culture was part of the healing pathway for Indigenous peoples on the whole, as efforts to reverse the damaging effects of assimilationist policies were increasingly being realized. This was also the era where the truth about residential schools was beginning to come to light, following the 1990 disclosure of Phil Fontaine (head of the Assembly of Manitoba Chiefs at that time) about his abuse in the Oblates of Mary Immaculate Residential School.[22] In Toronto, as elsewhere, the Indigenous community was steadily building culturally specific services and supports, knowing that this was the only way forward.

Having decided to live and be sober, Rene at first connected with Alex McKay, a street outreach worker with the Indigenous health clinic, Anishinaawbe Health Toronto. Alex set him up with detox, and from there he went for a brief stay at Na-Me-Res (the Native men's residence) on Vaughn Road. Rene had largely avoided associating with his Indigenous identity up to this point, but this was the beginning of reconnecting. He went on to Pedahbun Lodge, a Native treatment centre that had been operating out of a large house in the Toronto neighbourhood of Parkdale since the early 1980s. Rene stayed there for eight months.

With sobriety, Rene's gifts and talents returned. There is a photo of him standing in front of Anishinaawbe Health holding his first commissioned painting after graduating from Pedahbun. Rene began to work steadily again as an artist, while upgrading in things like microcomputer clerk training. He also enjoyed doing volunteer work, where he met Joan Bruder. Rene and Joan married in 1993 and moved to Guelph.

Planning and Planting (c. 1995–1997)

"The fifth stage is planting life, having your family, taking responsibility as a parent."[23]

In "Beginnings" Rene describes the birth of his son in 1995 as another critical turning point. For Rene and Joan, planning and planting also involved building their business of producing and selling Rene's art, which they have done ever since out of their home base in Guelph.

Doing (c. 1997–2018)

"The sixth stage is doing life: practise what has been given to you."[24]

As an Anishinaabe man, Rene's healing journey has involved re-engaging with Anishinaabe culture, and as an artist it has necessitated decolonizing his art and regaining his confidence to produce. This is the "doing" that he has been engaged with for almost thirty years now; a re-entering of minobimadisiwin or "the good life" in Guelph. Healing through art is thus a key theme throughout the book, and the reason there is a whole section dedicated to this theme (Part VI: Papawangani).

Rene has brought his spirit of lifelong learning into his art, as is evident through his engagement with evolving technology. In his story, "Renewal: Reconnection," Rene describes building his own multimedia studio in his home in Guelph. From this place, Rene continues to produce visual art, digital media, music, and writing. This is where you will find him most days.

In recent years, Rene's "doing" life has also involved working outside his studio as a teacher and mentor, which he attributes to not only growing older but also being part of a teaching clan, the Mizay, or Ming. As a teacher and mentor, Rene shares his stories and gifts with younger generations, as Elders do. He continues to be a regular performer, playing his pipigwan (flute), and speaks at festivals, universities, and community events.

Elder Life (Onward from January 2018: The New 70!)

"The Elder passes on knowledge."[25]

On a visit to his home territory in 2016, one of Rene's cousins mentioned that their community considered seventy the appropriate age for elderhood. Of course, being an Elder also depends on the knowledge you carry and how you comport yourself. Rene's definition of being an "Akiwensi" or "old man," is one who is bending closer to the earth. As Rene says, "I feel the thunder from the ground up these days!" Humour is never far off in Rene's version of elderhood, as can be seen on page 257, where his "new 70" portrait features him wearing a beat-up hat, cigarette hanging from his mouth (even though he doesn't smoke), and draped in an animal-print scarf—the result of him and Joan having fun one day and trying out a rock-and-roll hero look.

Rene now lives a comfortable and productive life in Guelph, and his sense of belonging in the city is supported by the connections he keeps with his family and communities online, as he describes in the story "Belonging." In that story, Rene also encourages his peers to take up "the new 70!"

As I was finishing up the work, I sent Rene this introduction for review. I will close with the email he sent back, which is typical of the wisdom, creativity, and optimism that my friend and teacher always brings. I hope readers enjoy visiting with Rene and gain as much from his storytelling as I have these last twenty years. Miigwetch!

Mon/6/12/2018, 11:19 am
Aniin Niidji
I'm pleased with the 'Intro' chum. LOL*!*
It reads like it's not going to be your typical memoir but
a real Anishinaabe storytelling tradition.
My mishoomis used to tell us stories like this by the campfire
because we would remember what he told us the last time.

What seemed to "trigger" his anecdotes was the way the fire
responded to the wind,
the lapping of waves, crows, pine smells, fluttering of wings,
bugs and of course, the picnic.
It's timeless. It's fellowship with Mishoomis and you're not lost.
Minawa apii,
Rene

A Few Words about Anishinaabemowin, Dialects, and the Use of Language in this Book

I am gete ombigedj, grandmother-raised at Pagwashiing, Longlac, and Aroland in northwestern Ontario, and I speak both the Aroland and the Longlac dialects of Ojibwe. There's a difference, and those two communities are only about 150 kilometres apart. Even Geraldton, which is only twenty kilometres from Longlac, has a unique way of speaking. So it's understood that traditionally your dialect defines the boundaries of your territory. The minute you begin to speak in Anishinaabemowin (Ojibwe), people know where you are from. If I spoke Ojibwe with someone from Cape Croker, they would know right away that I'm not from around that area. Even people on Manitoulin Island would know I'm not from there either. That's how we recognize our territories where we have stewardship.

Our language, Anishinaabemowin, is embedded in the land. Every rock out there, every island, every bend in the river, every river mouth has language, story, and history. With so many of our Elders gone, sometimes I feel like there's no one to give me a story. But the land still tells me a story; it gives me language, and you can still hear the territories in our languages. In those places where it's very rocky, it seems to me that the language is sharper. When I hear Ojibwe from Manitoulin

Island, they're really fast, almost like staccato. And when I used to talk to Basil Johnson from Neyaashingamiing (Cape Croker), I had to tell him to slow down a bit! Then as soon as you move towards, let's say, Sault Ste. Marie, it gets a little slower, and then slower still by the time you get to Thunder Bay. When you get to Winnipeg, that's where it really sings. I guess it's because of the prairie grass going back and forth. When I heard Norman Fleury from Manitoba talking Michif, it was a joy because I understood him, and it was this happy, singing language. But back home, it's more spongy, like mousse cake. It's all about lakes and rivers and rapids.

I'm particular to Pagwashing, as it's my grandmother's homeland, and the dialects there give me a sense of place and belonging. I suppose now that Anishinaabemowin projects are undertaken all over Anishinaabe aking, or land, there's going to be a giant push for consistency. But this could be another way of corralling our culture into a rez; at this internment place, Anishinaabeg will be fighting over consistency. It's control over our lives again.

The culture of Nookomis was disrupted when white people built a railroad through her territory and, after she died, they torched her house. I was left with no grandmother, no house—but my sense of place and belonging are still there, nested in the language of Nookomis. A whole teaching can even be remembered through things like baking frybread—in fact, I'm still learning the language through its recipe! I now realize that I've always made the mistake of preparing my frybread without first making the well or waanikanens. Making waanikanens in the centre of the flour in the bowl is fundamental. When I mixed baking powder, salt, and lukewarm water in the waanikanens, the ingredients formed bubbles. I never saw that before. Now I know why Nookomis made waanikanens, even though I thought it wasn't important. I took a short cut and my frybread turned hard and ugly. We must bizindan or listen—we must not take shortcuts in our language either.

Colonization has meant we live with the assault on our grandmother languages, and when something is murdered, its spirit wanders the earth looking for its body. Now, the spirit of Anishinaabemowin wanders the homelands looking for its body. As we call it home we can use various symbols to communicate our ideas, emotions, and desires. At one time, our communities on the land were autonomous and diverse and so we can develop our own ways of spelling Anishinaabemowin. No right or wrong way. Wherever the spirit of Anishinaaabemowin has found its body, a dialect is born. They may have torched Nookomis aadadj but she can find her house in you.

In thinking about language learning and revival I've also been chatting with my cousins from Longlac or Ginogaming. One expressed how he began learning the language through his prayers. The other said the same thing. He said that if he didn't know the Anishinaabe word that he wanted to use in his ceremony, he'd ask his ancestor and the word would be given to him. This revelation reminded me how I began to pray in Anishinaabemowin when I was in Pedahbun Lodge Treatment Centre twenty-eight years ago. Each of us has our own way back to Anishinaabemowin through the ceremonies and discovered something. We live it. We perform it. We pray it.

Now I'm thinking about teaching, and how it's hard to teach Indigenous languages in an urban setting because they are relational and need context. When you learn on the land, the land gives you clues. Land helps tie things together through dibaajimo, which means storytelling—you are tying something with the earth. When Nookomis took me out into the forest to snare or pick blueberries, she was speaking Anishinaabemowin, and now I can relate it to something else out there. I guess these days if I was teaching the language, I would have to find things to relate to in the urban setting. Maybe I could take people down by the river where I could find a way to connect.

One way I have been teaching in the city is through my work on Ojibwe word bundles, like the ones included in this book. Unpacking Anishinaabemowin words is like opening a gift, because if you break down the words you see a worldview. It opens my eyes and heart and gives me connection to the land.

I started working on these bundles years ago. I discovered this dictionary, written in 1834 by a missionary in Michigan named Baraga. At that time I learned that there are hundreds of dictionaries and grammar books about North American Native languages written by European missionaries as tools in their campaigns to supplant the Indigenous beliefs. So I decided to resist that campaign and decolonize the dictionary by working word bundles out of it. They Christianized, colonized, and stole our language to make it their own with those dictionaries. But they can be useful, so I intend to steal it all back. I ininigaade (hold in a certain way) the Ojibwe word bundles or Anishinaabemowin that my Nookomis Shebagabow taught me. Nookomis never knew a word in English. So liken the Anishinaabe words you find in this book to stones, each with a unique size, colour, weight, and shape. They were never bricks to be used to supplant our Anishinaabe worldview!

I think these Ojibwe word bundles are going to take me the rest of my life, but I'll do as much as I can to pass them on to the younger generations. Our Anishinaabe youth have their visions and dreams, and hopefully an old guy like me can dream along with them.

PART ONE

Odinimanganikadjigan
Stories of Nurturing

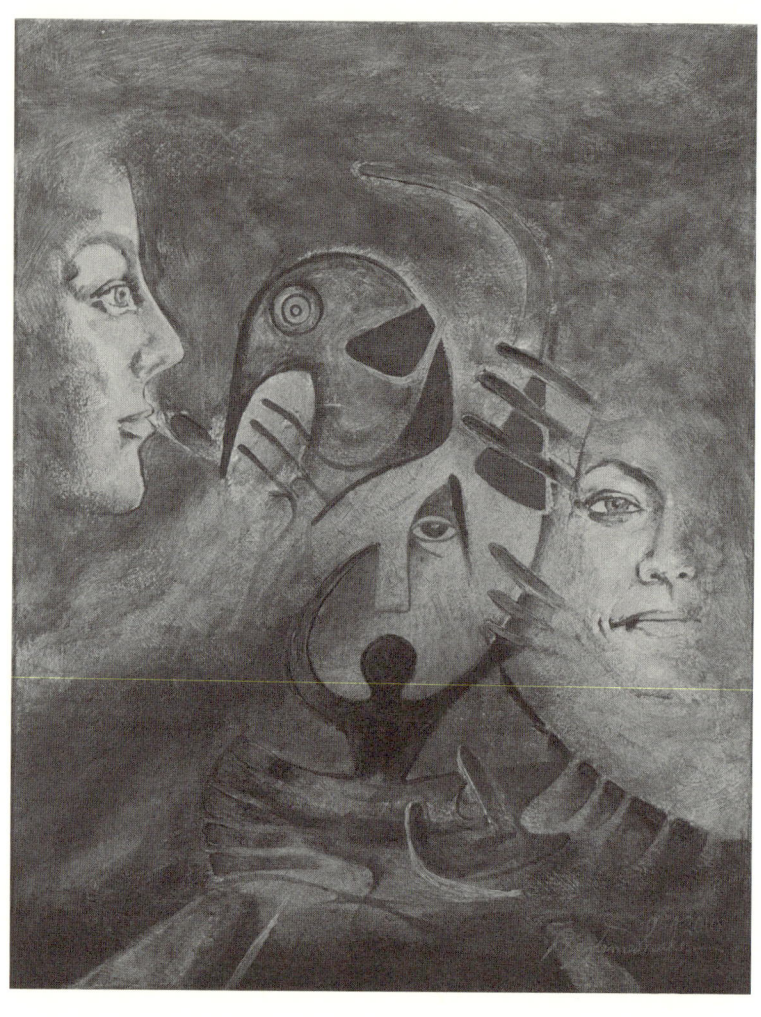

Odinimanganikadjigan, Birchbark Canoe Headboard, 2011, acrylic on canvas, 40.6 x 50.8 cm.

Odinimanganikadjigan

Odinimanganikadjigan, Birchbark Canoe Headboard. Odiniman-
gan (shoulder), nikadjigan (headboard).

Miigwetch apitchi indinag weshkatchi Anishinaabeg. Kawiin wiika
inda gikenimasig Odinimanganikadjiganak.

Mi wigwasi-jiimaan ondji mashkawag. Indigo abita'oonag kinji-
inowag dash. Gegiin giishkijiinigok Odinimanganikadjiganak.
Miig gaie eshiwebak, mindimoieg gi zhawenimishwad giibi niigian.
Nookomis ngi nitaawigi ig. Ni zhaabwii!

I give thanks to the Anishinaabe speakers. This word
"Odinimanganikadjigan" gives me the true meaning behind the birchbark canoe headboard.

The headboards serve to strengthen the hull at both ends of
the birchbark canoe. From there, the gunwales extend out to join
like hands in the middle of the canoe. You get a warm feeling as if
Odinimanganikadjigan is hugging you. This is a metaphor for the
matriarchal society that I was blessed to have been born and raised
in. My grandmother gave me a community that shaped my faith and
character. I am a survivor!

Boozho,
Greetings

Nenewe (male); boozho, or wabos (rabbit).

Boozho comes from the trickster's name, Nenabozho. The trickster is half man and half rabbit. We honour the trickster in our greetings.

Adisokan,
The Tradition of
Storytelling

In today's society, storytelling is separated from day-to-day living. You go for a few hours of "entertainment" and then return home to your real life. It's put in a box. But when I was a kid, storytelling was something that happened while you were cooking food in the fire pits. You might roast a moose under the sand with rocks, and that was eight hours of waiting—and so, storytelling. Stories could also be shared when you were smoking meat or fish, as you had to stay all day to maintain the right amount of smoke. In that lifestyle, the story only ended when it was time to eat! That's why as kids we were always around the fire. The grannies would be making the stew, or smoking something on racks, and we would respond by drawing maps of little men hunting along lakes and rivers in the clay. The girls would make model villages with tents, always getting us boys to play the dad or the baby.

Sometimes while my grandmothers were sitting around the fires, the stories would turn dark. Famine was a big thing, and there were stories of times when there were no rabbits or partridges. But hard times were always seen as part of the rhythm of life. Those hard stories would be shared, and then all of a sudden the grannies might start laughing with something that began, "Remember that old guy . . . ?"

There were "professional" storytellers who travelled around our communities, too. The guy who did this was called the adisokewenini. His job was to repeat, to relay, to add to—to thread the communities together with story. He had to be young because it required living on your own: hunting, camping, repairing your canoe and snowshoes, looking after your dog team, making your own toboggan. So he was pretty well-versed and he had this huge responsibility.

My grandmother used to talk about those guys that did that. She said one time the uncles were very sick and this adisokewenini came along. He saw the situation and asked, "What's going on here?" Then he asked the women to make some partridges for a feast. "They need to eat," he said. He got everybody to eat, he got everybody moving, and then the uncles got well. I think the healing came from the stories that went along with the feast, and the women cooking. Shay shao tao, he called it.

The adisokewenini is the one that moves around, then, and he moves things too. You see, he's into healing of all kinds. He would get your muscles moving, blood circulating, and everything. This sometimes involved using humour—he did that. And then when he was expected in another community, he had to go. It might be 80, 100 miles away.

There's no more guys like that. Today we have these storytelling festivals and people that travel around. I sometimes do that, but I'm always telling stories just as part of my life, too.

Oongona Gaming

I come from northern Ontario. Just look 200 kilometres northeast of Thunder Bay and you'll see a place called Aroland. That was my father's community. It has an Indian name that means Spring Water Lake Portage. In Anishinaabemowin you'd say *Oongona gaming*.

Oongona gaming was a gathering place, a rendezvous for families who had been trapping all winter. They came home to this village every spring, where they renewed ties with old friends, buddies, and people they had grown up with. There were always some marriages happening and it was a great time for festivities. We would exchange gifts. There was even a kind of religious feeling involved in being a part of the land and celebrating life. Oongona gaming was also a very beautiful place, with a spring water lake that was perfectly clear. In the summer it was the colour of turquoise. There was a CN railway line that ran past there, and at some point, someone decided to call this place "Aroland."

My first home was a log house on the grassy hill near the swamp in Aroland. I remember a couple of times when that swamp tried to take my life. One night, my parents took us to a dance and on the way my dad dropped me into it. It seemed like he was just watching me drown! (Years later he told me that my grandmother, Nookomis, was furious with him.) Then another time, I was on the boardwalk and I just fell in. I heard the bubbles and murmurings of the swamp. I didn't know how to swim but I thrashed and kicked my way to the top. I walked home no longer afraid of the monster in that swamp.

It's interesting because here people ask, "How old are you?" Well, there's no such thing in our language. We say, "How many winters have you endured?" We celebrate how many winters someone has survived! This is because winters were a very hard time for people. Game was sometimes scarce, and families had to separate to go to their respective hunting grounds or trap lines. They split up into small groups of two or three families because of the game. So we always looked forward to spring—when the ice broke up and allowed for visiting. That was the time to get all "slicked-up" and comb your hair with bear grease or goose grease so you could look like Elvis Presley. We were excited to see all the other families as they gathered at the portage and imagined what girls we would flirt with and date! It was also a time to exchange hunting stories. We would build fires and talk and go to square dances.

All these things I'm writing about have to do with celebrating life. There was a sense of gratitude and thanksgiving that families had survived another winter and endured the hard trapping season. We only trapped in the winter, because the summers were a time of plenty. There were berries everywhere: blueberries, raspberries, strawberries, moose berries, cranberries, and cherries—and many other wild plants to eat. We planted potatoes. We were sick of meat after eating it all winter; we were full of it! We just wanted to eat fresh fruit and berries because that was a treat.

Living in harmony with nature means you can't afford to make mistakes. Let me give you a picture. One time I was out with some friends who had two dogs. These two dogs went after a groundhog who didn't have time to take refuge in his hole. The dogs tore apart the poor animal and snapped its neck. Here we see Mother Nature at its best; I guess the domesticated dogs reached way back into their misty pasts to hunt and kill for their supper. One mistake for the groundhog and he's history! So it was the same way with life on the hunting grounds because we needed to survive, and mistakes weren't covered by life insurance, workers' compensation, unemployment insurance, OHIP, and such things. Any disrespect for lakes, rivers, ice, and even your tools, like the axe, meant death. Out in the bush there aren't any ambulances to come and get you. No highways, no telephones, not even a two-way radio. So you really had to know your stuff, your Native stuff.

We were always told to respect fires, and you depended on your family and your life-long partner regarding the fire hazards that came along with your camp. The tent was made of canvas and was coated with oils for waterproofing. The airtight heater was like a tin can and too much heat inside the tent was bound to cause an explosion. Another fire hazard had to do with our bush glue. I remember seeing my grandmother repair her canoe with gum she had stripped off the pine tree. When the tree was still standing and alive, she would scrape all of this hard, hard gum off the trunk with willow sticks. Then she would hold this gum over the fire until it started to melt and drip. I can see her now, pasting this melted gum over the canoe and moving back and forth to the fire and the canoe. If you made a mistake the gum could ignite. It was highly flammable; it could burn the whole canoe and take your life!

There were lots of other lessons about respect, including the respect for trees. We never cut down all the pine trees, because they provided more than warmth. That gum was important—we even chewed it as a natural tooth paste (but the taste was awful)! I would call this technology; it was a way of using Mother Nature to meet all of our needs and an interdependent relationship developed.

Outside of Aroland were my paternal grandfather's hunting grounds, called akiing (on earth). Those lands were passed down to him from his grandfathers before him, as we Meshakes were stewards of Murky Creek country. We never say ownership when referring to these territories, because how can you own something that was given to you by the Creator? But each family was a steward of a particular part of the country. The families lived there in harmony with the plant and animal life, including their wolf brothers, moose brothers, marten brothers. We always addressed bears as either mishoomis, grandfather or nookomis, grandmother. When we heard the wolves it was tremendously moving; like meeting another tribe or nation of people. We lived side by side with them with mutual respect. So when they were in a pack, they never crossed our paths; they would just walk beside and then go somewhere. And when we saw a wolf we said, "Hey Nisayneh!" Hey brother, how are you?

Lately we see that our animal brothers are becoming fewer in number. Back home it is related to the clear-cutting. I don't know what the fur-bearing animals are going to do to keep warm—grow longer hair? Before, there were plenty of trees and shrubs and willows for protection; now there's nothing. It's almost like a desert.

In all of this, I can still hear my grandfather. When the trees were standing, he'd point to them and say, "They are my life, my heart, my soul." I think it broke his heart when he saw the same places years later and everything had been clear-cut and slashed and burned. He died a few years after that, maybe from that broken heart, and when he died, I guess a whole culture and tradition went with him.

That was the lifestyle we experienced as families in the bush; we spent many, many winters hunting and trapping and snaring to feed ourselves. But we always took only what we needed from the land, not what we wanted, but just what we used. That was instilled in me, and I still practise this today in my everyday life; just taking what I need and leaving the rest for everyone else to share.

Debisiwin, Sufficiency

Debisi (sufficiency or abundance); win (state).

Debisiwin lies in the heart of our Anishinaabeg homelands, it's land-based economy, it's creativity. Get our hands working! For example, Anishinaabeg artists labour to inspire, elevate, enlighten, and heal. Our practise is debisiwin.

Eden

Eden, you impress
me with your new cotton sundress,
and your face
delicate with jade earrings and necklace.
There's even better compliments
without these adornments
when I open my eyes
in Gichi Manido's paradise.

Aki,
Earth

Aki (earth).

Put the Anishinaabe word Akikodjiwan, which describes a dangerous whirlpool, next to Aki, and you get an image describing a globe. The Old Ones knew the earth was round!

Pabeshuh gejiguhkeeng, Human Being

Pabeshuh (one by one); gejig (companion); guhkeeng (on earth).

In my research I came across this word for human being. It describes the uniqueness of each human being in the companionship on earth.

Pagwashing

My strongest childhood memories are of a place called Pagwashing. Pagwa means to open, and shing is a place. Pagwashing described the pockets of lakes that sit among rolling hills in my maternal grandmother's traditional territory. Maybe at one time there was a huge river going from James Bay down to Lake Superior, but much of it had dried up, leaving an underground creek that ran like a thread through the land and connected the lakes. Pagwashing was this watershed; lakes that were green or bright blue, so crystal clear and pure that we drank from them.

I lived with my grandmother, Madeline Shebagabow, in Pagwashing after my parents were sent away to a tuberculosis sanatorium and up until the time that I was sent to residential school. I was just about four when I went to her, and that's why I can say I was gete ombigidj: grandmother-raised. Nookomis homeschooled me in Anishinaabe language, arts, and culture. At alternate times, she would enroll me at the Long Lac Indian Day School or Aroland Indian Day School. My cousins at Longlac, Ontario, often wondered why I was still very smart when I came back from the bush. They didn't know that I had attended Aroland Indian Day School as well. I often did the three schools in a year.

Nookomis was registered with the Long Lake #58 reserve, but she moved around a lot and lived mostly on her traditional land. She refused to be confined to a reserve. If we were at Longlac and Nookomis said, "Okay I'm going to go to Pagwashing," my uncles might reply, "Uh, I don't know if we can anymore"—because they hadn't designated Pagwashing as a reserve and we were being pressured to stay on the rez. But she just ignored that. She'd leave and then we'd all end up in Pagwashing. That seasonal mobility still existed.

The community in Pagwashing was built alongside the creek that snaked under a CN railroad track as it headed down toward McKay Lake. About fifty people lived there in our odena, our village. There were log cabins and tar-paper houses as well as houses made of boards that we got from the section crews who were always maintaining the tracks. The CNR had made a two-storey house for the crew boss, and we got other leftover materials from there, or from the railroad sheds they built to store their pushcars and tools. If you worked on the railway you also had access to lumber because the steam locomotives used a lot of wood. We had a log house, but my grandmother preferred living in a tent, or a wigwam.

Our houses were never partitioned—just one big room with the kitchen on one side and a table in the centre. But everyone had their own space; every family their own corner. The oldest always had a particular space in the lodge, like Uncle Robert, and of course my grandmother, who had a certain area that we stayed away from and respected. Some kid might run around, and then "Uh-oh, you're in Grandmother's space, get out of there quick!" These spaces were also workspaces. My uncle repaired his snowshoes or carved his paddle in his space, my aunt had her own corner, and us kids did too. It was a like a big room with a bunch of invisible rooms. Other than that, there was no electricity, no running water, nothing.

That's the kind of community it was. Railroad tracks and big sandy pine trees. Blueberries growing wild all over the place. I have memories of smoke in the air, bingisige, because every evening people would light up their fires and make a smoke. The whole place was smudged, but it was for mosquitoes. Then everybody modishiwe; visited and shared tea, stories, and laughter.

The only decent wage in those days came from working for the CNR on the railroad. Some of the men had steady jobs, but there was still money to be made from fur trapping. In any case, we didn't need much money. We had rabbits, partridge, moose, beaver—there was a lot of meat around. In the summer we ate blueberries. You didn't even have to pick them—they were just there! So when I was a kid there was no welfare dependency because everybody worked. I learned early on to snare and skin rabbits, and that if I wanted to eat, I had better get a rabbit, or go fishing. If I wanted jam, I had better go and pick berries. I learned to cook scones and other stuff. But my grandmother never forced me into anything. I started getting water for her and chopping wood at one point, though she liked to do things for herself too.

I remember Nookomis cooked a lot of rabbit. You know the rabbit gut and all the greens that are there? She used to fry that up. That was my vegetables; the twigs mixed in with the green stuff from the way the rabbit digests. It was already broken down, so it was easier for us to eat. I liked the rabbit brain too. Sometimes we would get a big blessing of fish, like a whole bunch of suckers in that creek, but after a while you would get fed up with them! We knew the practises of other fish runs though, and when the whitefish were spawning, that was another big feast. We'd go to the rapids and camp on one side where we fished and netted and smoked whitefish.

There were usually bears on the other side, because that was their territory, and no one camped over there. They never came across and we didn't go across either.

Speaking of territories, I have one memory of going into Nookomis's tent when she wasn't home. I wanted a slice of bread and found a whole loaf of bread wrapped in a red and white package. I unwrapped it with care and proceeded to dig a small hole through the end crust. The inside tasted so delicious that I ate the whole thing but left the crust intact. I carefully rewrapped the hollowed loaf of bread and put it back. I didn't want Nookomis to know who ate her bread. My Dad told me many years later how Nookomis almost cut her fingers off slicing her bread. She said, "Waabiganoojiinhs!" She told him that a mouse had been into her bread. (She knew it was me.)

Another memory I have is of my grandmother doing a healing. We were in Pagwashing and she was so sick she said, "I'm going to build my lodge right here," and then she built a lodge right inside the house. She was teaching my aunt Christine how this was done among women. She went inside the lodge—a sort of tent inside the house, all wrapped up with tarps like a sweat lodge. I sat outside watching them. My grandmother was inside, and Christine was sitting by the door smoking. They were praying. They had those big enamel basins in the lodge; I guess there were rocks in there. After that my grandmother was healed.

In the midst of this Anishinaabeg life, there were other people living and moving along those CNR tracks. That's how we got around before highways, and Nookomis and I travelled all over by train. I have a strong memory of the time my grandmother, the chief, and I took a train to Port Arthur (now Thunder Bay, Ontario) to see a dentist. I didn't know what a dentist was. I was all alone in the room with him and the strangers cloaked in white. I cried out loud for my life. I cried out loud for Nookomis. I cried out loud when they tried to smother me. I cried out loud into the darkness. I awoke from the darkness in the arms of Nookomis. That smell of chloroform triggers the terror that I felt to this day.

Nookomis had lots of friends and relatives who lived along the tracks; often women who had married the lonely crewmen or section foremen who worked for the railway. The men were mainly French but there were also Italians and Irish men and there was a lot of intermarriage. My dad, Jeno, was even named after an Italian my grandfather had worked for on the railways. Over in Aroland we had lots with last names like Therriault, Banniault, and lots of Legardes, and then if you went to Thunder Bay you got a lot of Scottish and Irish, like the McGuires. They were built, with tattoos all over. It was okay if they fought each other, but if you got in there, forget it—you were dead. All this activity had been brought in by the railroad, which our people had also been working on for some time. My great-uncle had even worked on it all the way to Regina.

Nookomis made money from the railroad by selling blueberries along the tracks. The trains would stop, and our women would trade fish for tea. The matriarchs loved Hudson's Bay tea—that was like gold! They also loved satiny or colourful things they could make kerchiefs and clothes with, and especially sainebas, ribbon. There were pots and pans and stuff too.

During the war years there were German prisoners building the roads, and even a Japanese internment camp, called "Camp 2." Nookomis called them "the tea makers." She said the white people had told her to shoot any Japanese we saw: "If you see a Japanese run away, kill them!" they said. But Nookomis wouldn't have had the heart to do that kind of thing. "Why should I?" she'd say. "They've done nothing wrong." My dad also had stories about working alongside Japanese men when he was cutting logs for the steam locomotives. He said he had a Japanese friend that sharpened the saw he used when cutting wood for the trains.

Nookomis could also talk about guys who they met walking along the tracks during the Great Depression. She said that our people would feed them and help them on their way. I guess some would call them hobos. They were just passing through, and apparently were very respectful—they had their own code of honour. I think many of them were saved, actually. That kind of history is never talked about.

Gisiss,
Sun

Gis (heat); iss (from).

Heat is linked to energy. Nookomis saw heat, saw energy, not only light!

Ogiminan

I think the highest form of respect in our homelands was reserved for the grannies—women like my Nookomis. This was likely because they were the matriarchs. They were not only Elders, not only grandmothers, not only women, but they held the culture together.

I often think of what the word Anishinaabe means. Anish: to lower the man. These names ground us! It implies that women were always here. And us guys, we need to be put in our places, I think, to have that balance. Then there's aki, which means earth. But akina, that's where the mother comes from.

When I address the Creator, I also say akina, which means everybody, and to me, mother. And when I say agiway—it is to return to earth. Becoming the earth, together, or one. That's mom.

You know the word "ogiminan"? That's mom too. There's that ogi in there, which means mother, and the ogima is to manage; there's all these little spaces and you manage them all. Ogima is boss or president or chief, and ogimakwe is the female version. So some say ogimakwe for the older women who manage, but I prefer ogiminan, because it's just who they were. Either way, that word is telling us that the mothers were the leaders of the nation—that was their title. But somehow our words got corrupted along the way, because I started to hear words like "Anishinaabe ogima," referring to the Indian agent.

When the Europeans came to make treaties, we had our grandmothers with these ogiminan authorities. Our people were confused by these men who came on their own. Where were the women? Then they introduced Queen Victoria, and we thought, "Well, that's their great-grandmother. So they must have an Ogiminan too, who sent them." We made treaties with her. Unfortunately, the Europeans at that time had no respect for women—not even for the grannies who were our authority figures. The matriarchs were not asked to sign the treaties. They were ignored, which put the men into an uncomfortable role.

When I was a kid, I often saw my uncles defer to the matriarchs. Whenever there was a dispute between them (which was bound to happen, living close together as we did), they would go to their mothers. The mothers would make fire and sit by the water, the lakes and rivers, and talk about things. The matriarchs were the ishkwe— the fire. It was like a court, a settlement of disputes before it got violent or out of hand. After the grandmothers talked, they went back into their homes and would talk to their sons. That was the judgment or verdict. And my uncles would have to live by that.

I remember that my grandmother's authority was tied to her traditional name, which was Kitchi Gabwik, the one who is standing firm, standing fast. This name really did describe who she was as a person and delineated her governing role in the community.

Nookomis was definitely steadfast. I remember one time she told my uncles, "Okay, I'm going to pick blueberries today," and my uncle said, "Mother, we planned on going next week."

"I'm going right now," she said. She just took the tin down, started packing, and away we went. I was dragged along no matter what, but I was happy to go out picking blueberries. We left in our canoe and paddled along the lakes and rivers to this beautiful lake called McKay Lake. We set up camp and the next morning I heard this small little *put put put put*—a three-horsepower motor—that was my uncle arriving. Next thing you know, everybody was camped on that island, picking blueberries. The other grannies came too, saying, "I'm going to go where she is. Pick blueberries too."

Nookomis stood up to the restrictions that were placed on us by the Ministry of Natural Resources when they were forcing us out of our traditional territory. The old matriarchs like Nookomis still camped wherever they pleased and set their nets where they wanted. And when my mother was in the tuberculosis sanatorium and Nookomis wanted to see what was going on, she just pitched her tent outside. She even stood up to the Canadian National Railway. There was this one time when she had gotten on the weigh freight with some family. They had loaded on their canoe but were short on money. When they told the conductor, "We'll pay you when we get to Longlac," he threw them all off. That's when Nookomis put a curse on the CNR. You just couldn't push my grandmother around.

What happened to that matriarch system? It was a government—a way to come to some sort of treaty between the uncles so they wouldn't be fighting or involved in violence. But when we were moved we lost that land-based court system. The government put in the chief and council, and the men became chiefs. We were colonized, and it was like disturbing a mound of ants. You know, it's like they all live under the cover of a big board, and if you remove that board the ants are scattered all over the place. They have to rebuild somehow and be resilient. But there's a power in being gete ombigidj, old lady–raised.

I talk a lot about my life with Nookomis in Pagwashing; it's the setting in all my books and it's in my art. And when I was running my small business, selling art and writing or doing presentations, it was always the middle-aged women I felt most at home with. I always felt respect, working with older ladies—even the church groups, the Lionesses, the IODE (Imperial Order of the Daughters of the Empire) ladies. I think I liked working with older women because in the '50s when I was growing up, the matriarchs were alive. They were powerful, and there was a lot of manaadendamowin—respect.

Those grannies, they continue to discipline me today, even though I am now over seventy!

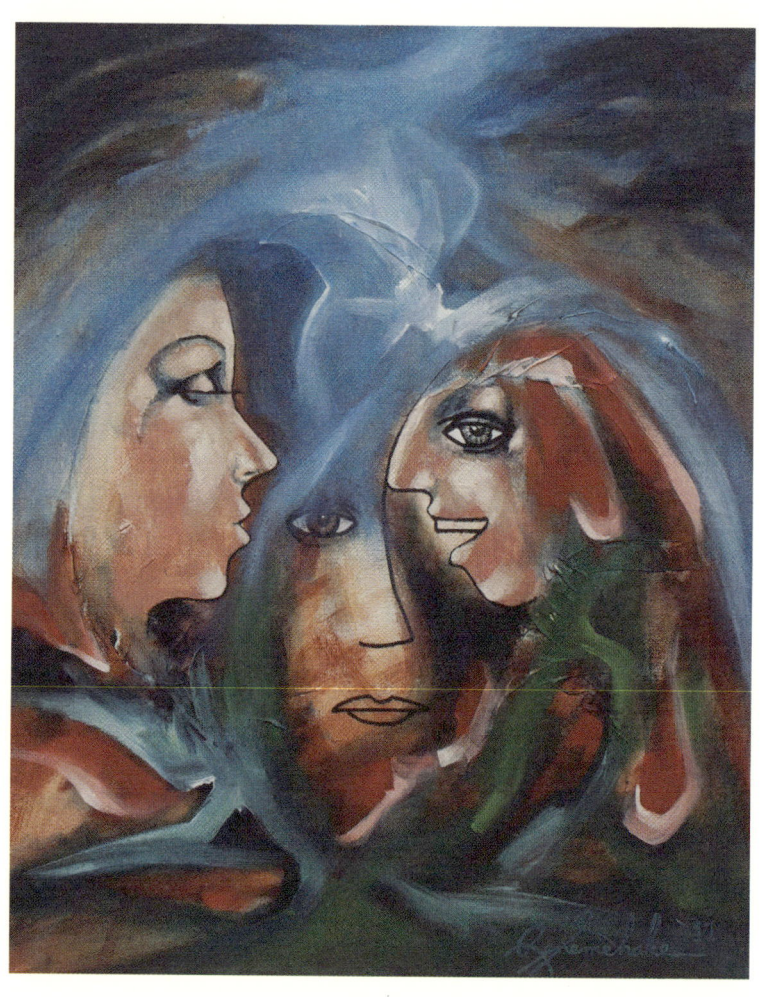

Gekek, Hawk, 2001, acrylic on canvas, 40.6 x 50.8 cm.

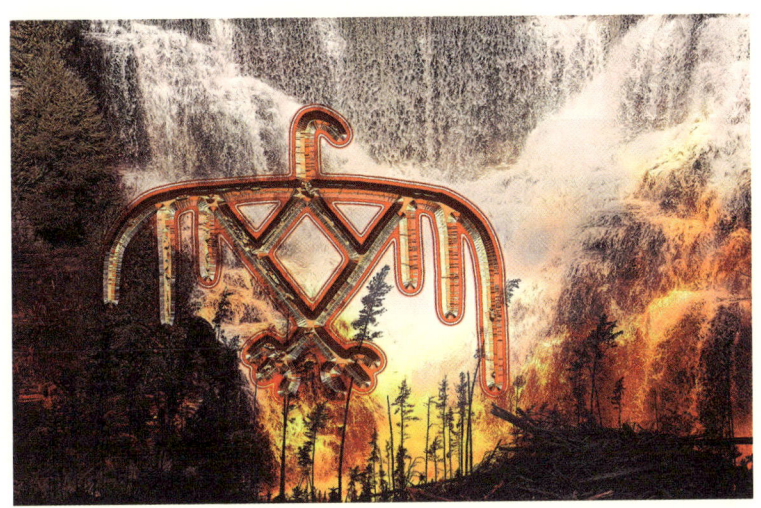

Manidowishkang, Spirit Walker, 2018, multimedia art.

N'zigos Christine

I held her hand,
bone, lumbered and tanned.
Her storied pulse told
of stars new and old.
Though pale and small
underneath the blanket shawl,
full of woman and sword
of battles scored
notch by notch,
yet tender to the touch.
Ah, N'zigos Christine,
Nibaan and dream
of us, that trail behind
you've come to find.
Lead us back to the sun
like you've always done.
Locked are my eyes
to see you rise
Splendid in your regalia,
Singing—Hallelujah.

Ikwe or Ishkwe, Woman

Ishkote (fire); kwe (woman).

Ishkwe comes from the word for fire, and fire is the symbol of life. Women are Life-Givers.

Minowegijig

In the summertime, when the lakes rose to their respective watermarks, we used to camp on the shoreline and I would play on the beaches. The memory that stands out the most from those times is of Minowegijig, my great-uncle, as he was making preparations to go moose hunting.

Minowegijig was weakened by Kennedy's Syndrome, so I never saw him walk; instead, he would crawl on his hands and knees. But the grandmothers would put him in a canoe and the lake was his freedom. Minowegijig: mino means good; nowe is speak, or voice; gijig is sky. Speaking with a good voice; it explains who my uncle was. I always found him to be a spiritual man and had great respect for him as an Elder. And I was impressed by his relationship with the animals that sustained us.

I remember one evening, when Minowegijig became very still. He reached for his gun case and his beautiful .30-30 Winchester—what he called his "tirty-tirty." But before he unpacked the gun from its case, he began praying and speaking to the moose with his vision. He was explaining what he wanted to do with the meat, the hide and the bones, and his wife was praying along with him.

I was fascinated watching this ceremony unfold; Minowegijig then slowly unpacked the rifle handbreadth by handbreadth as if he were skinning the moose. He continued with his monotone conversation with the creature, and it even soothed me. You see he was Minowegijig—he was talking goodness into his gun and the moose. He started humming as he took out some rags and polished the barrel, trigger guard, and butt. He cleaned the bore of his gun as if he were skewering out the marrow of the moose's long bone. When he was done, the rifle had power and purpose; to ask the moose to give up its life for the Anishinaabeg families. It was ready. The agreement was fixed.

The night was drawing in, and so Minowegijig said "Ahow!—let's go." That's the kind of relationship my great-uncle had. He knew the timing. Even the winds—you don't want to go out when it's windy. We call that niitaga, when there's a calm in the evening. So he got into his canoe with his wife, along with my grandmother, her sister, and me. Minowegijig sat in the front of the canoe and his wife was in the back.

After we had paddled awhile, Nookomis, my grandmother, said, "Shaamashkiin!" (duck or lower you head) and we saw a moose raise his massive antlers from the waters. The waters gleamed and rippled, cascading off his shoulders like a big waterfall. My grandmother ducked and so did I because we did not want to startle the moose. We continued along, stopping our paddling when the moose rose from the waters, and then paddling again when he dove to feed on the weeds. As we drew closer, the moose rose one last time and very leisurely walked away from us. My great-uncle took aim, shot, and the magnificent creature crumpled on the shore.

All the grandmothers jumped into the knee-high water and we started tying it up. Then we towed the moose across the lake to an island. The grandmothers made camp, butchered the moose, and started a fire where they could put up racks to smoke the meat. There were families camping around the lake like they did every summer, and all were invited to join us. Then the practise of maada'oki (the redistribution of wealth) took place. Everybody was happy, they all came ashore and each family was given a portion of the meat. That's the Anishinaabeg version of income tax.

This kind of sharing happened in the dead of winter too. My grandmother and her sister would say, "Let's go set some snares." They would build a special toboggan with skids on it for Minowegijig. The women made the trail first. Or if we were fishing, they pulled him to the lake. They would put him out on the ice and he would start chopping with a big long stick. He would chop one hole, and then another, and another.

Then he would tie his net and send out the stick from one hole to the next, asking the women, "Is it there yet?" I don't know how they did this—the currents underneath could have carried the pole anywhere. But they found it and it didn't take them long to get a whitefish or trout. And Minowegijig fed the whole community with these fish.

Minowegijig understood that you could not amass wealth for yourself. Maada'oki meant the difference between good governance and tyranny.

My great-uncle Minowegijig taught me about the appreciation of food, the ceremony of harvesting, and the respect for the animals who give themselves up to us.

Dodawa, Treat

Doda (carry out); dawa (to him, to her).

It seems dodawa comes from the word dodem (clan). A clan is honoured by how they treat others, not by their status in the community.

Minawako; Mishoomis and the Economy

I once asked my paternal grandfather, Ambrose, how he met my grandmother. He said that guys from his generation travelled by rivers and lakes and portages, all over north of Lake Superior and down to Thunder Bay. He said he had his own canoe and a couple of dogs and food and tents. He'd meet his friends along the way because that was their highway.

When he came through Spring Water Lake Portage (Aroland) the people living there would welcome him. They had a protocol called "Biwide," where you treat this visitor like a VIP. So Mishoomis was Biwide in that community. He said he saw this young woman there and thought that sometimes they mistreated her. He didn't like that and so when she got older, he came one day and told her "Miiwe ashi odapininan (Come with me, my canoe is out there)." My grandmother happily went with him.

My grandmother's family had always moved around too, all the way up to the James Bay area. You see, Aroland was never a settlement; it was just a portage where people settled. There was no odena, no central place until the Aroland Logging company (1933–1941) built a trading post there. That building eventually became a one-room schoolhouse. I went to Indian day school there as well as in Longlac, and to this day, when I smell chalk it reminds me of that old schoolhouse in Aroland.

I have lots of memories of that school building because my grandfather had a general store "next door"—just half a kilometre away! His life as a businessman evolved from the time when the Aroland Logging company was also nearby, with big barns by the river and stores, run by a Mr. Reid and a Mr. Russell. I guess those were the ones who taught my grandfather how to be an entrepreneur. When the stores left with the logging company, Grandfather started his store.

Like lots of Anishinaabeg, Mishoomis was known by his nickname. In Aroland you didn't call him Me(i)jakigijic. He was known as "Abozingwe." Aboze means greasy; greasy-faced guy. Maybe as a kid he had a greasy face. Or maybe it was because sometimes we used lard or grease on our faces as an insect repellent; maybe he overdid it!

Abozingwe was the first in everything, like when he got this old army truck. There were no springs in that thing; when you got on you bounced all the way to your destination. He also had a big black horse and one of those chuck wagons with giant wheels; he used it to haul water or when we went to pick blueberries. I think eventually that horse was on the railroad track and got hit by a train. It survived but it got sicker and sicker with some kind of infection and they had to shoot it because there were no horse doctors around.

At Grandfather's general store you could find groceries, clothes—you name it. When Anishinaabe were hungry they'd come to see Mishoomis and buy things on credit. Then they would go trapping and sell their furs to pay off their debts. Mishoomis also bought pine and spruce cones and resold them to Kimberly Clark as seeds for their tree planting.

As a kid, I was most impressed by the cellars in Grandfather's store—you could keep cool there on hot summer days, and everything was down there. You could drink your Cokes, Orange Crushes, 7-Up, and of course your pastries were also down there. Sometimes there were beautiful tin boxes that you could drum on too; I used to jam with my uncle Cashimere on them.

The store had an adjoining pool hall where Mishoomis hosted dances and gatherings. I don't remember a lot of drinking at the dances because Anishinaabeg weren't allowed to drink; those who wanted it had to go to their white friends or the bootleggers in Nakina. That was another economy; people trading moose meat, geese, or fur for a case of beer, and there were people making their own booze too. All this developed because if you wanted to buy liquor you had to give up your Indian status and become an expired Indian. One of my cousins actually enfranchised because he wanted to drink. When Treaty Day came around there was money, and everyone would go see him for booze. "There's my treaty money," he would say.

Sometimes drinking was part of the economy when Mishoomis hosted fur buyers from out of town. There is a story about how one time they played a joke on a fur buyer that always came around. They said that Mishoomis was counting the furs, and a few of my uncles stood by as the fur buyer said things like, "Oh—that's a nice one—a big beaver . . . thirty dollars!" They were drinking, and one of my uncles was doing the tally. Then when the fur buyer would pick up another fur, "Oh—twenty dollars"—the uncles would give him some more to drink.

That fur buyer turned into a really happy drunk, and you know what my uncles did? When my grandfather picked up a fur and said, "Otter?" the fur buyer replied, "Oh—an otter—ninety dollars!" Then they took the ninety-dollar fur and put it back in the uncounted stack. My grandfather said, "Minawako," and they wrote the ninety dollars down on the tally.

I don't know how long they did that for, using the same fur. But I guess they eventually felt sorry for him, telling each other, "That's enough money." Then they packed the furs away.

I wonder what happened when he got home? I guess he always sold them for double what the Anishinaabeg got anyway. "Minawako," was all my grandfather said; which meant "they are doing it again and again."

PART TWO

Nibinaabe
Stories of Warning

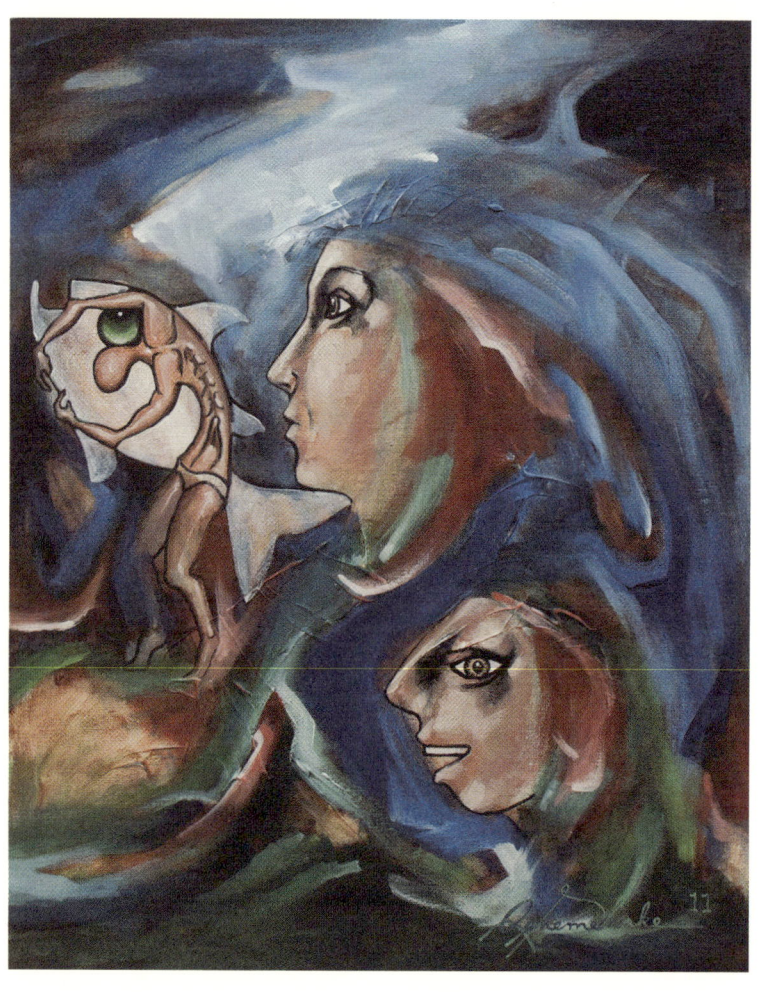

Nibinaabe, Mermaids/Mermen, 2011, acrylic on canvas, 40.6 x 50.8 cm.

Nibinaabe,
Mermaids-Mermen

Nibinaabe, Mermaids-Mermen. Nibi (Water), naabe (being).

Megwa nibi gibi binagaming, Nibinaabeg ki mino-inawemawan amikwag. Amikwiishing gishi gaazowag. Miijimika gaie. Nibinaabeg gaie amikwag gi wiikondiwag apane. Bakaan gibaakwa'iganikewadj bagamigidaazowag, miidash ga ishi ishweiag wiikondisiwin. Gomaapii, waniikenaniwan Nibinaabeg ga ishidjigewad.

Nongom dash, danitaagoziwag, aiaangwaamissiwag!

In the time of clean waters, the Mermaids-Mermen were great friends with the beaver. The beaver dams provided places to hide from large predators. There were abundant freshwater plants for food. The Mermaids-Mermen and the beavers held many feasts. But when the Builders of Concrete Dams came, the feasts stopped. And gradually the Mermaids-Mermen name disappeared from the Anishinaabe stories and were forgotten.

But some of us have begun to remember and to listen to their warnings!

Traps

It seems to me that we—the Indians—built the Hudson's Bay Company (HBC) and we got nothing back in return. There is an interesting story my grandfather used to tell about piling beaver pelts the length of the musket when the traders were buying. Well, the muskets kept getting longer and longer!

There were all kinds of traps that came with that HBC relationship. There were those ones that the Company used to provide us with—connibear traps. They were spring operated and big enough for your head to fit through. They could also break your arm in half if you didn't know what you were doing. I remember my father telling me about a wise old beaver who knew how to trip these traps. He would hold a stick in his mouth while he was swimming and he could likely smell the oils on the new trap. He'd set off the trap and so was impossible to catch. I guess he died of old age eventually. He must have come from a long line of experienced and wise ancestors.

Some traps were harder to escape. For example, when you started out for the trap lines, you stocked up on basic stuff like flour, baking powder, lard, rice, oatmeal, barley, sugar, tea, and anything else you needed. There are fierce winters up north; you had to be equipped and prepared. These things were bought on credit, so you were basically in debt before you were gone. Of course, the store managers were always happy to give us credit, and it became very hard to break even. And naturally, they always threw in a couple of bottles of booze.

Crazy water, firewater, alcohol! People all over the world have figured out their own way of making alcohol, but my own people chose not to have it. This wasn't because they lacked the idea or the technology. It seems to me it was more of an effort to avoid introducing that substance into life. It was around though. I remember my grandmother used to have these huge birchbark baskets filled with blueberries, and because we didn't have any refrigeration, these blueberries would start to ferment after a few days. The word is bogejeday, and it describes the bubbling action of the sun and the heat on the fruit. But this was thrown away. I suspect the medicine people knew about alcohol, but it was never revealed to the people. They observed each plant and the powers it held, and maybe they also observed what happened when the bears ate our fermented berries.

There's a word for drunk—it's giwashkwebi. It means that your mind is turned upside down or you are disoriented or delirious. It describes the action of having that fermented juice. So anything that touches our society with giwashkwebi was hidden. It could be abused, but it could also be used for medicinal purposes. But when alcohol was introduced as part of the fur trade, it devastated a way of life. It caught us—another trap.

Bataadowin, Crime

Bata (I damage, or wrong myself); ataado (trade); win (state).

There is a trade in wrongdoing. There is a price! The damage that you cause will come back to you in due course.

Bug in a Lampshade

A fly had come
to lie dead
at the bottom
of the frosted bulb and lead.
He'd been the bug
zipping by the good life
free of boast and smug
and unceasing strife.
Now out of body, his spirit pursued
the hum in the lampshade so dire,
fluttered, and followed
the filament and big wire.
Unclean things and spirits
battered his resolve
the more he whizzed over the merits
of a lighted glass bulb.
Once he forgot
the hiss and snakes
up he shot
through the turbine intakes.
The hum stopped to churn
as he hovered in vain
only to return
to the frosted bulb again.

McIntosh

March 19th, 1967.
I checked the article again.
March 19th, 1967,
the year the school burnt down.
For me, McIntosh never burnt down.
Back then,
Brother J, my Supervisor's
petting impaled my body
to the dormitory bed.
Disembowelled, I died.
Old J had a little lamb
Branded it Twenty-Three
Old J sheared its wool and skin
Its fleece grew filthily
Twenty-Three won't graze no more
Graze no more along the stream
Twenty-Three was unworthy to dream.
From the article,
I clipped the picture
of the white, three-storey residence.
I ran outside, broke a cedar branch,
and set the bough and clipping ablaze.
As I stoked the fire,
my body emerged from the burning page
to reunite with me.

Get an Education

After Indian residential school I went on to Westgate Collegiate in Thunder Bay. I was probably the only Indian there, but by that time I wanted nothing to do with Indians, nothing to do with my language or culture. I had that fear—and yet I was very comfortable in an all-white classroom. I could give talks, even write an essay and read it in front of the class. I had a good time performing.

Just before I graduated, I was getting restless because there was no challenge for me anymore. I wanted to do things like build racecars with all the colours! One of my friends in Geraldton owned a car repair dealership. He said, "You can come and work here." But I didn't have that high school class; in any case, that wasn't exactly what I wanted.

It was around that time that I heard about hippies in Toronto. They were strict with our dress code at Westgate and we weren't allowed to wear our hair long. So this hippie life in Toronto sounded like freedom to me. I walked into my high school counsellor's office and said, "I'd like to go to Sheridan College." He grabbed the phone right away and called Sheridan: "We have a Native student here . . ." All they wanted was a couple of drawings from me. The school gave me lots of paper and I started drawing like crazy. Next thing you know they were putting me on a plane. It's like a door just opened. *You're free, Rene, get on this plane!*

I remember landing in Toronto—man that place was big! I met my counsellor in the airport; this guy from Indian Affairs, and he drove me all the way to Brampton. It was like a city that never ends, and I kept thinking, *where are the hippies?* Then when we got to the Sheridan College campus it seemed like a small place, not too impressive. It looked more like an office building. I met my teachers first, and then the Dean and then I finally saw some hippies in the cafeteria. The best part was when I saw this guy walk in with a green leather "Lands and Forests" jacket on. I said, "Hey man, where are you from?" "North Bay," he responded, and I came right back with, "Hey, you're a fellow northerner!"

He was a Metis, Philip Papineau. We started talking about fighting fires, all kinds of things. That made me want to stay more, because I was scared; everything was new to me. Eventually we got to be very good friends, and this helped with the terrible homesickness. It was a good thing that he was around, too, because he was better with the girls. I couldn't let anyone get close because of the abuse—I didn't want to get betrayed again. Sometimes the girls were hurt; I could see that. "I'm sorry—I thought we were just friends," I'd say. But then Philip would come along; he'd fix things up. He'd flirt with almost everybody. He was the opposite of me. I always thank him for that.

As for the hippies, well, they seemed more interested in me than I was in them! They all said, "You're the *real* man. You're beautiful!" I'd get everybody listening to me . . . *wow man, that's so cool.* But I didn't know what the fuck I was talking about. One of the girls said, "You're one regular nature boy, aren't you?" Another guy spoke up, "You're the osmosis." I didn't even know what that meant; I had to go to the dictionary—"Hey Phil, you got a dictionary?" They would talk like that, smoke some more stuff. So I had plenty of college hippies—even the teachers were hippies, with their long hair and their English accents.

Then we got our own commune going. My Indian Affairs sponsorship gave me $90 a week for spending money, and because all my other expenses were paid, sometimes I'd use my money to help a student meet their rent. "There's more where that came from," I'd say. I became a little bank, and it felt good to help others.

I don't know how we got any work done or graduated in the end. We each had our own small cubicle studios, and someone would always have a bottle of wine. I'd have a bottle of whiskey or a mickey— and we would drink and paint at the same time. *Wow*—"Put Jimi Hendrix on and crank it up!" We'd think our art was so great, because the more high you were, the more every little stroke became very significant. Philip decorated the room by painting it dayglo colours, and sometimes we'd just sit and watch a Salvador Dali painting. Or we'd turn the sound on the TV off and keep different music playing while I'd paint. CCR, Jim Morrison, Janis Joplin; all those hippie songs. Everything was surreal.

My dad had said, "Get an education; your job will be waiting for you." Okay, Dad. So that was my college life.

Gichitwaawis, Elevate

Gichi (great); twaa (action), wis (influence).

Living in community has two effects. Either we get elevated to work for the good of the community or we suffer the consequences when we do not. Gichitwaawis now!

Andjiidana Gitodem

One time the court workers needed a translator, and so they came to find me in the bar. There was a visitor on trial; lots of times there were these older guys from outside our community and they would get charged with hunting out of season.

My grandmother had always taught me to treat outsiders with respect and think of them as Biwide. Biwide is a visitor, and there's a VIP treatment that goes with that. Biwide is just passing through. You give him food, lodgings, respect. But they were bringing me to court to ask if he was "guilty" or "not guilty."

As I was walking along, I started thinking about how I didn't know if he did it or not, so how was I going to ask the question? I was also really uncomfortable because he was Biwide from the north, and my grandmother had taught me that many of these northern Elders had powerful medicines.

At the time we had this habit in our community. A phrase would go around for awhile. "Begosha, asha gagibiti'ainin." That means "Don't, or I'll plug your butthole with my fingers!" That goes around, like a word bundle, and then it goes away. Anyhow, there was this expression going around: "Andjiidana gitodem," which was interpreted to mean, "Did you do it as a prank?" And that's what went through my head when the court workers came, because I didn't know how to translate "Do you plead guilty or not guilty?" Sometimes when you're drunk you think about lots of stuff.

I kept laughing about this thing, "Andjiidana gitodem." It also implies, "Did you fake your dodem?" It was funny, but it wasn't funny, because I knew about dodem, or clans, and their responsibilities. It has to do with whether you did it on purpose—but it's not that. "Did you do it as a prank" is the closest. And then there's that word dodem: "Did you dishonour your dodem?" Because whatever you do in our culture in terms of your behaviour, you're honouring your dodem. It's self-governing. It gives you a conscience.

So the teachings have a way of influencing your behaviour. How you behave is your dodem. When people ask you, "What do you do?" Dodem is what do you do.

Anish endodamaan is "What are you doing?" You're asking, what is your dodem? And if it's me, I'll tell you I'm from the Mizay, the Ling fish clan. I teach.

So then there's the judge; if he says yes to the judge, then he's guilty. That's another worldview. So this guilty thing—we don't know how to say that.

I soon realized that by asking my question, Did you do it as a prank?, the person couldn't win. If the person said, "Yes," it meant that it was just a prank to him. But the court would take it as, "Yes, I am guilty." But if he answered, "No," the court would understand it as, "No, not guilty." But in my mind, the "No" would mean that he wasn't joking; that he knew he was dishonouring his dodem and doing wrong.

So I didn't go. In any case, I was still drunk when I got there. I walked away. I had to respect this old guy, who was Biwide to me. I had enough Grandmother in me to say, "No, don't do it."

Dashinge, Gossip

Dashi (as often as); shinge (spread out).
    Dashinge used repeatedly spreads out and divides community.

Migoshkasitagos, Controversy

Migoshk (poke or trouble); kasitagos (with words).

    You get a picture of controversy as a poking or stabbing with words.

Policing

In the old days, we had a clan that would police community. It was probably Bear Clan, but there were other kinds of police clans. They not only policed the community; they policed spirits. Now we have rez cops, but they forget one very important job—to police the spirits, like Windigo. Today there's a big question of missing and murdered women. I was thinking one day as I was out for a walk about what's happening to these young women. Then I was thinking of this Windigo spirit. It steals, kills, destroys. There is a word for that cannibal: Gadjishwesh.

Windigo is very different from Missaabe. We can get along with Missaabe. Missaabe is Bigfoot. Sasquatch is the West Coast term for him; the Anishinaabe call him Missaabe. Missi means grand. Missisibi means grand river. Then there's "aabe," like Anishinaabe—so it's a being. See that "aabe"? So put them together—missaabe—and he's just as real as anybody else. I think it's more respectful that he stays in the periphery of the camp or lodges. Missaabe is not like Windigo—it's the opposite. He's the spirit that represents honesty. One of the seven grandfathers. So my grandmothers knew about Missaabe. But when you say that word "winis"—winitchiged means filthy, unclean spirit.

Windigo has allies too. Inevitably, Windigo will turn on its own allies! Where are these guys that are responsible for this violence? Those targeting the women are allied with Windigo spirits, which makes them hard to catch, and you cannot police spirits unless you have this knowledge. Your Bear Clans are supposed to teach you about these spirits. That's what's missing now; traditional people like that. So we've got to go back to that kind of knowledge and that you have a choice. How do you restrain the filthy, unclean spirits that possess some guys in our societies right now, among us?

This extends even to water. "Wiinaagamin" means polluted water. See, what's happening on our rez is that we have this polluted water. That's Windigo at work. So we've got to start to do something about this spirit knowledge, or maanidoke; you've got to dig really hard. And when I start to look at this it gets very dark; there's even some things that I won't mention. There's some things that I don't want to talk about. It's very dangerous if I expose too many things in my story or artworks. It's about what could happen to others. Not to me, because I am protected. I take great comfort knowing that you will "reap what you sow." Or Shaakitamaso! I have angelic helpers that minister to me. But to talk about these things in general, somebody else might pick up on it and go into things that they don't understand. I'm afraid of that. So all these things have connections to polluted water and filthy, unclean things and the policing of spirits.

So if part of the problem is police not caring or working hard to find these women, that's the Windigo spirit in the system. Maybe the police don't know such things. And because we're marginalized, that kind of world isn't allowed or known in the justice scheme of things. "Those crazy Indians; they don't know . . . ," that kind of thing. They just put us in jail—and you're worse off when you get out. Nothing's changed. It comes back to the disturbance of this matriarchal system that was there to police everything. That was there to govern even the Windigo spirits.

Then there were other things that happened in our policing type of systems—like gabiindige'ig—that's the curse if you disrespect a stranger. Biwide is a visitor but there was a protocol related to when a stranger was visiting from another community. You don't know what medicine they carry, and if you disrespect them you'll enter into this jiisakaan or shaking tent. That too is a dark thing or a good thing. It can be a bad kind of lodge. The jiisakii (practise) is to build this shaking tent; then you put a curse on someone. It's not like that other lodge I hear about—the midewiwin (the way of the good heart—a grand lodge). It's a different kind. It could be that the one you disrespected would set up that jiisakaan, and jiisakii means you enter that jiisakaan, in person or not.

When I was in McIntosh Residential School, these Anishinaabeg from across the lake would come and visit us every now and then. They were old guys and they'd come because we had these movies. Or sometimes they'd just show up and play hockey with us. One time some of the kids were being very disrespectful to one of them. I knew the man as a Biwide. Those guys were powerful, and I respected them. Then I heard one of the Biwide say something about "should we or should we not?" I knew right away what they were thinking about. That guy could have made jiisakaan and put one of the kids under. When I heard it, it brought back memories from my grandmother's teachings about respect for Elders. Respect for Biwide. Then I heard the other Biwide said "No—Kawin." See, he made the decision there not to do anything with the kids.

I don't know what happened after that, but maybe that's why McIntosh burned down. I was grateful they didn't do anything. But because we're being colonized so much, I think I was the only one who saw what they might have done.

Then there's another one—the Maansokaan. My grandfather talked about those guys. They're a bunch of Anishinaabeg—scaring the living daylights out of people and stealing their food. They're like a gang. They make these strange spooky noises. To startle or maanso. They made these strange sounds in the bush. So suppose you were camping by the lake. You had your lodge and your food, all your fish drying on the racks, your tea, your belongings. Everything. You're just living. Then you start to hear these strange noises . . . but you're not sure. It's unnerving. I don't know what sounds they made. Just to startle you. The sounds they made were growls or howling but they were spaced out to terrorize you and shiver like crazy. Ooooh . . . Maanso! Sometimes wolves do that too. If you hear a wolf howl, it goes through your bones. You start to shiver and the howl passes through your body. Rattles your bones and shakes your heart—you're all shook up. They were professionals—to go maansoke.

But you never saw them. They were probably young guys, but they were like ghosts. It would take a lot for you to run away from them—get into your canoe and paddle across the lake and by the time you get back your food was gone. Their purpose was mischief. Have fun with someone. You intimidate them; frighten and threaten them. It's a sort of psychological warfare. My grandfather said they originated from the west. I guess that's the lighter side of things. They're not violent. When you consider it, it's like a drama. I never heard of them taking a life.

My grandfather used to talk about other things, like what happened in the jiisakaan lodge.

When he was a teenager he remembers my great-grandfather participating in this shaking tent. My grandfather said, "I watched them building this shaking tent—this lodge." He wanted to go in but his dad said, "He's not ready—kawin." I guess after a time they built another shaking tent and this time my grandfather was a little older and he asked again, "Can I go?" His dad said yes. My grandfather said he went in expecting to hear great revelations about life and wisdom and all the things he would possess in his life. And he looked down and his underwear started talking to him! I don't know what it said, but that was it!

Treaty Day

AGWANAAMON! The word seems to be a refrain from a chorus in a song. But it was never a song. The refrain was chanted at the annual Treaty Day for us Anishinaabeg. The Indian treaty party came by a CNR train with X-ray equipment. Then we lined up for chest X-rays. "Agwanaamon!" I heard the X-ray technologist say. After my dose of X-ray, I was paid my treaty money of four dollars. Being too young to understand money, I let my grandmother take care of it. But by the time that I understood money, lead aprons, and shields for my eyes, the annual X-ray train had been delayed. If I ever hear the word AGWANAAMON again, I swear . . .

Ancestors

Haze of asawa-shoniia, gold
and wood smoke racked my lungs.
The riverbanks faded, but behold
how giggles mocked the fiery tongues.
'Haw!' cautioned Manitowadis. I grew quiet to reminisce.
On the seventh winter of my life, I found this deserted village where
bugs quivered, shivered on the waters. As the night swallowed them,
I told Nookomis, my grandmother, about the ghostly, wooden crosses.
"Bego wiika miinawaa izhaa ken imaa!" said Nookomis. She raised
her right hand and crossed her heart. Then she began, "Long ago,
Chibaie never before suffered, visited our odena, but his smallpox over-
whelmed us. The more that we tried to keep our dying young men
and women warm with his blankets, they kept vomiting."
Nookomis
Gone was her bliss
Burned her blanket,
Burned her tears and birch basket,
But not Chibaie, the Smallpox Revenant I was never
supposed to meet.

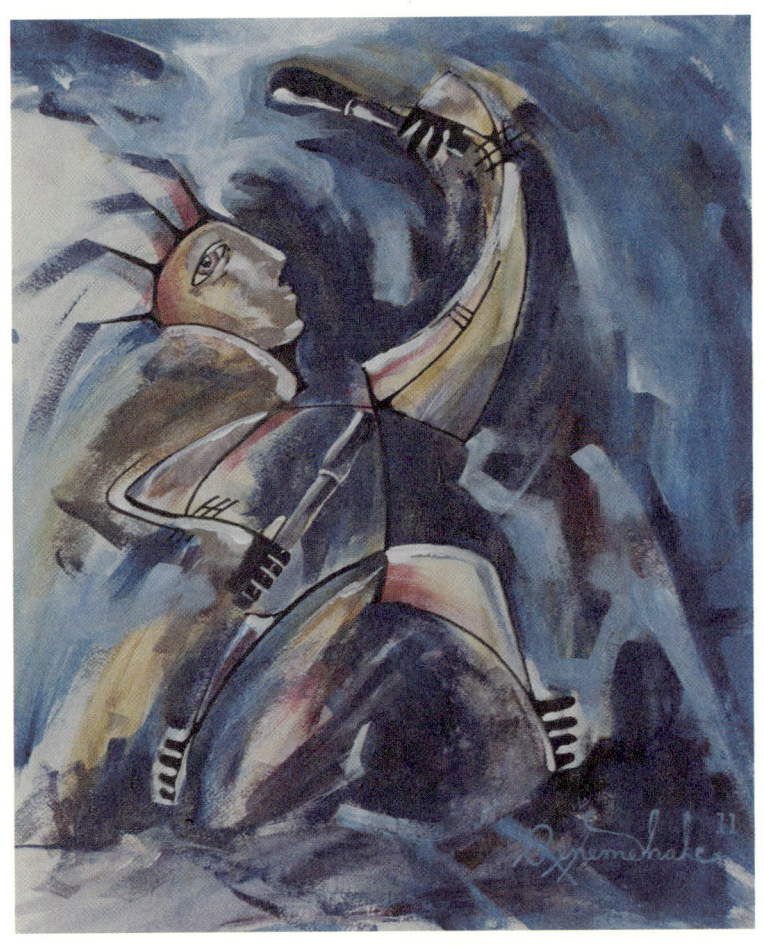

Teweige, Drummer, 2011, acrylic on paper, 35.6 x 43.2 cm.

Lake Nookomis

Nookomis.
Let motor oil fold
and tar this
wing and bird.
Mix your drink
of pesticide
cocktails and sink
in the hydride.
A toast to algae
and drown, stark
of life and tally
on the watermark.
Mikwam glaciers
trumpet call.
What chilling acres
await us all.

Odena, And When the Heart Stops Beating

Odena. Ode means heart, and odena is the village, the place of the heart. The heart of the village needs to pump, to breathe and move. At one time we had this when we moved with the seasons. In the summers, Nookomis's people all gathered at Longlac, and then in the fall everybody moved away to their respective hunting grounds. We'd move in and out of Pagwashing because that was my grandmother's territory. That was the real bush. Pagwashing is not a reserve—it's a real odena. But Indian Affairs kept on trying to get us to move to the reserve.

"You can go to school here; we'll take care of your kids." They told my grandmother they would give me a lot of clothes to wear to Indian day school, and that as long as I went to school we'd get all sorts of rations as well. Sometimes my grandmother would go to the Indian agent and say, "I want some clothes for Rene," but it was like she was bribing him. "If you don't give me some clothes, I'm going back to the bush, back to the trap lines!" Then they would give her a voucher for the Hudson's Bay store. I would go to Indian day school for a while, with my school uniform from that bargaining. Sometimes Grandmother got things of her own—like bundles of cloth. She made shirts, blouses, whatever she wanted. She really loved the spools of twine to make fishing nets, and those nice shiny knives too. Then we would go back to the bush, and the Indian agent would keep promising my grandmother this beautiful house on the rez. "Move to Long Lake Indian rez; we'll give you a house, clothing, food, and Rene can go to school."

The matriarchs held out, and there were guys too that hung on and still moved around a lot too. Even in later years when I was fighting forest fires, we'd hear these gunshots and we'd say, "That's Old Legameway." You couldn't tell him he was hunting geese "out of season," because that was his territory. There was another guy, Old Man Moses, who lived on Hardrock. You could hear his gun go off every now and then, and you knew he had got something—moose or partridge, or geese or ducks, in and out of season. We'd say, "That's Old Man Moses." Even the game warden understood that you couldn't put these old guys in jail; they might shoot. Old Man Legameway eventually died and Old Man Moses kept on until he got really old and had to move to the rez, where they took care of him until he passed.

Eventually Nookomis had to move to the rez because the grannies started dying off, and then, while I was away at school in the late 1950s, the government burnt down all the houses in Pagwashing. That was to make sure we stayed on the rez and became welfare dependent.

When they moved us onto the reserve, that did something to the uncles. The government had burnt my grandmother's house down; that, among other grievances, was something the uncles couldn't express. But it all came out when they were drunk. So I always felt false when I went to the reserve. *That's not how we do stuff.* I saw aunts getting drunk at Christmas, and uncles getting drunk, and I would think, *What's going on here? What's wrong with my world? They don't do that at Pagwashing. They're more respectful to their wives and everybody else. More in control.* Entering the rez and seeing people hammered, I saw the mockery of a man. It wasn't long before I became that. Ashamed.

Those things that I saw hurt me to this day. When we were living on the land at Pagwashing I never saw my aunts being beat up by anybody, because the grannies would step in. There were arguments, but nobody had black eyes after. There were no broken bones, ribs or anything else. And remember, there were no hospitals, no ambulances, no telephones, no cops. Everything there, every person had merit because we depended on each other to stay alive. So if you beat up someone, the whole community will die. There was this interdependence of everyone. If one hurts, all hurt.

With the forced moves, Indian Affairs reversed the roles of grannies being in charge. On the reserve, the men got to be chiefs, and pretty soon you had guys running the place.

Others, like my uncles, were taken off their lands, and those men that were so strong out there in Pagwashing now become very docile. Something terrible had happened to our matriarch system; that way to settle things, like coming to some sort of treaty between the uncles so they wouldn't be fighting or engaging in violence. There was no more land-based court system. It was like turning a cup of tea upside down. So you're drinking from a cup that's upside down all the time.

Now we call Longlac, the town of Longlac, Odena. It's as if the heart left and moved to the town. And then we call the town of Geraldton Odena. It's a bunch of white people. But we don't call our own village Odena anymore.

Widji-bimige'idimin, We Are Neighbours

Widji (together); bimige (lodge side by side); idimin (speak to).

This word teaches that we speak to our neighbours. Sadly, we do not speak to our neighbours to stay healthy anymore.

Gaa-Bamashiwadj,
Sky People

Gaa (they); bamashi (fly along); wadj (beings).

I was watching TV and thought I heard the Anishinaabe word Gaa-Bamashiwadj used in a sentence by a Cree from northern Quebec. Our Anishinaabeg ancestors knew the sky people. Where do you think Thunderbird comes from? WAKE UP, my Young Ones!

Lens Cap

Have you ever been to Agawa Canyon? Agawa is an Anishinaabe word meaning shadows. Out of the shadows and up high, rock paintings in red ochre appear, facing Lake Superior.

First, let me tell you what happened to me. I took my new family to northwestern Ontario to introduce them to my relatives. I had just bought a Contax camera and rolls of film for the road trip. It had a Carl Zeiss lens and all. Liked it!

When we got to Agawa Canyon, we left our car at the parking lot and climbed down a steep path to the rock paintings. Once below, I noticed broken pipes poking out of the rocky ledge. The government had built a steel fence to keep tourists from falling into Lake Superior, but the waves ripped them out. I knew it was done by the Spirit Custodians of the Agawa Canyon paintings.

Because the ledge beside the cliff was narrow, I carefully photographed the paintings above me. I watched where I was stepping as I cautiously angled my shots. Once finished, we went up to the parking lot. I opened the back of my camera to retrieve my film and guess what? The roll of film wasn't there! Empty! Gone! I distinctly remember loading the film in my camera.

The thought of going back down there to photograph the paintings once more did not please me. I went back with bad blood. To make matters worse, the lens cap fell out of my camera and into Lake Superior. I thought it was going to float. It didn't! The lens cap zigzagged all the way down into the depths and disappeared. When I had done photographing, I had my new roll of film intact.

I drove away satisfied. Then it hit me. Ah! The Spirit Custodians of the Agawa Canyon had taken my first roll of film and my lens cap in exchange for taking photographs of the paintings. I considered how much I've lost being an urban Anishinaabe—I should've offered asemaa, tobacco, before I took anything from Agawa Canyon.

Gikiwe'on,
Flag

Giki (mark or sign); iwe (there or yonder); 'on (transporting someone in a canoe).

Pictographs depict flags waving on canoes. Friends or foes?

Migadiing, War

I dreamed I was told
Be redeemed
and go write in bold
about migadiing, war in the land.
I stood before
the migadiing land.
I searched all around
the wind speeds and sand dunes. When from the ground,
a sunken wedge impugns
through its shrouded rust these letters
of encrusting rust—U.S.
I swear I heard Migadi Spirits say,
"It's scary, Go pray!"
This dream kept me affright,
I haven't slept,
but prayed all night.

Ininashawaganak, Messengers

I drove to the hills. A place that has inspired me to write poems. Yet, it's been a mystery to me why my writings were always brief and tentative. In the same place nearby, there was a firepit for hosting Sacred Fire ceremonies. It was during our ceremony that a dear friend and I identified the firepit as the bowl of the pipe, and the old maple tree, the stem of the pipe, and together they formed a living Grandmother Pipe: Kokomissiw Opwaagan. This was the second time that I've met Kokomissiw Opwaagan since I was five or six. I'll tell that Kokomissiw Opwaagan story in Part VII.

With great caution, I sat down on a log. I began to focus on the fire pit. The sun was on my back. I remembered the time that I smeared wood ashes on my face and walked home. Man! Did my grandmother give me the lecture of my life. Being five, I only understood that it had something to do with death. Never did it again. Was there ever an Ojibwe funeral tradition where you'd wear ashes on your face? I can still hear my grandmother saying, "Gida shiwis! (You will be cursed)."

As I was reminiscing, a tiny translucent emerald jewel appeared on the rim of the firepit. I was enchanted even more when the firepit resembled an amphitheatre. At once, the jewel moved and split in two. I thought, bugs! These bugs were either mating or cannibalizing each other. I kept watching. Time passed, then another emerald bug like them appeared. It scooted up and dislodged them. The bugs scattered and hid from each other. One bug rushed to me and I said, "Come close to me and I'll crush you!" It stopped and bathed in the sun. I admired the metallic green, so emerald on its tiny back. A living gem, I thought, and what are you trying to tell me?

When I rose, my tiny emerald ininashawaganak messengers disappeared. I took one last look at the remaining Messenger on the ground and it flew up and vanished from my sight.

As with visions of mine, if you walk away feeling anxious, it's a bad omen, and if you walk away feeling elevated, it's a gift. Well, I felt elevated. The connection between the emerald ash borer and the Emerald Isle was staggering. The Spirits of these lands mandated me saying, "Don't be afraid of your words," and, "Your voice is free to write your own stories based on your grandmother Kitchi'gabwiik's teachings."

The experience took me back to the time that I met Kokomissiw Opwaagan when I was five or six. Now at seventy-one, she and the emerald ash borers tell me that my voice is free.

I've been fasting from alcohol and cigarettes for the past twenty-nine years in my vision quest. Visions have a language. The signs, symbols, and meanings come from a world that's teeming with life. It gives breath to your voice, and once understood, it builds real life relationships.

They tell me that the emerald ash borer kills ash trees. It's non-native, invasive, and a green menace to Canada. But no one tells me about the forest industries clear-cutting the boreal forest of my northwestern Ontario homeland.

PART THREE

Wikwedong
Stories of Loss

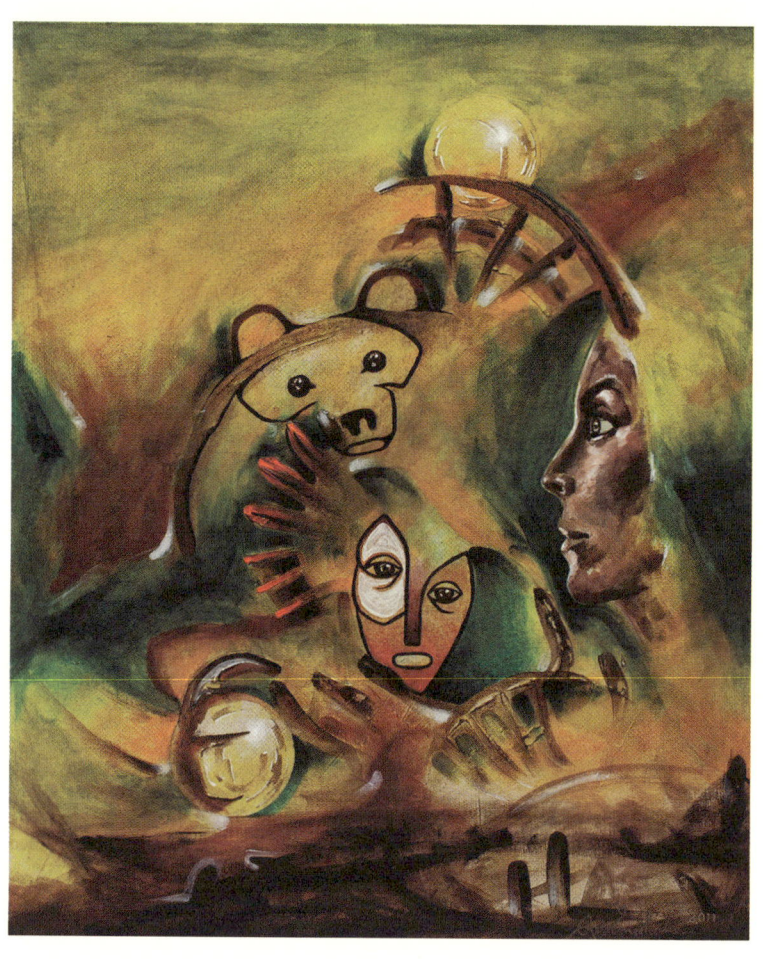

Wikwedong, Wikwedong Bay, 2011, acrylic on canvas, 61 x 76.2 cm.

Wikwedong

Wikwedong, Bay. Wikwe (bay); dong (in a; from a; to a): In a bay.

Ngi oshki noondan Wikwedong megwa Ningaa gini madjad Fort
William Indian Hospital Sanatoriuming. Ngi windamag, "Nga bikiwe."
Gawiin dash gibikiwesi. Ngi wabama abading. Biwidensing ashinagosi.
Awenen? Nda gwedjimik, "What grade are you in?" Meshkwat, Ngi
bagitina assinikang giba datagabid. Odisabandang nash Wikwedóng?
Miinwa g'madja. Angoding dobiskaki. Indasswashin dash omondi
assinikang asha nanimidana daso biboonong ni masinitchige.

Ni masinitchige dash, Ningaa kang ondji.

I first heard this word "Wikwedong" when my mother left us to
go to Fort William Indian Hospital Sanatorium. She promised to
return but she never came back. I only saw her once. By then, she was
a very small stranger. Who was she? She asked me what grade I was
in. I let her lean against a rock and left her gazing out across the lake.
Did she see a healthier Wikwedong? Once again she left us, promising to return.

I've been leaning against this memory, this rock, for over fifty years,
and painting through my mother's eyes.

Chingwan, Meteor

Chin (short time); gwa (fall); an (fly).
The flyer that falls for a short time

Angel in the Falls

Torrents drape your body.
Cascades thundering till you discern me, liquefying
and snaking down your face.
You flick me from your misty embrace
to the depths to plumb.

Kishadisiwinok

I was born in 1948. They say that my mom took me out of the Nakina hospital within the following hour and into the January kissina, cold. Women were tough in the day. Mom was tough through tuberculosis, fatigue, coughs, and blood.

When I was about three years old, my mother went into the tuberculosis sanatorium, leaving my younger brother Kenny and me. My dad followed her, but we weren't allowed to go. Mom promised to return after the coughs and sneezes stopped. She still wanted a family and gave me Veronica and Ralph while she was gone. When she sent me pictures of Veronica from the sanatorium it gave me dreams! Dad eventually recovered and they sent him back, but Mom was in for the rest of her life, moving from the Indian hospital sanatorium in Fort William to Gravenhurst, and finally to where she died in Winnipeg in 1960.

Mom ran away from Gravenhurst, and that's how I got to see her once in all those years. She came home to see her mother, my grandmother Kitchi'gabwiik, who was raising me. I think my uncle Biidan got her out. He was her brother and they used to write letters. He knew she was on the train, and when she got off he brought her back to our house beside the big church in Longlac, by the shoreline.

When I saw her, she was very, very tiny, and there was no kind of connection. I never hugged her. I remember thinking, *who is this stranger? I don't know her*. The family said "Rene, that's your mum." *Yeah, okay*, but I never felt anything. I didn't know who she was really. That's what happened there. And when she got back on the train to go to Winnipeg my cousins said, "Rene, why aren't you crying?" *Crying about what?*—You know? *Leave me alone.*

I didn't have much to do with my mom that one time she came back. I remember she had a doll—I think it was a Barbie. I played with that thing, trying to make it walk. Mom said, "Only girls play with toys like that." I didn't care; I just enjoyed making it walk around.

She was with us for a few weeks before the RCMP came looking for her. They took her and put her on the train and then she was gone.

I never understood the abandonment at the time—that was a new terror, I think. I never realized how much it would impact my life until I went into recovery at Pedahbun Lodge. It was there that the tears came right out. It was abandonment—I had to deal with that, and those women sitting with me at Pedahbun said, "Let that go. Let your mother go, Rene."

Dawaa, Space

Da (be); waa (spread out).

 The universe is spread out. It's also a gap.

Off Limits

My hair has been off limits to the world for a long time; taboo ever since I graduated from Indian residential school. From then on, everyone was prohibited from touching my locks.

At McIntosh they would keep shaving our heads. *Here comes Brother Jasmine and his clippers.* All the hair gone. Everybody had a brush cut, every single one of us—the small boys, my cousins, the middle-sized boys—even the girls had a bob cut. Then when I got to high school in Thunder Bay I heard about hippies. I heard that they wore their hair long and dressed any way they wanted. My school had these monitors telling me to tuck in my shirt, button up my shirt—so when I heard about these hippies in Toronto, they dress in these flashy bell-bottoms and wear their hair long—*yeah*—*that's where I want to go!*

There's white people that love to tell us about how they had a great-great-grandmother who was an Indian. So I say I must have had a great-great-grandmother who was white because my hair was curly when it started growing again. When you see my mother's picture, her hair was also really curly. I have a memory of my mother that one time I saw her after she ran away from the sanatorium; she kept wetting her fingers to smooth her hair down at the front, but it kept curling up like crazy. As for me, I used to put a lot of grease in my hair to straighten it. You ever see Jim Morrison's hair?—That's what it was like—I'd part it in the middle.

Finally I was able to grow my hair long when I left Thunder Bay and went to college, and the girls, holee! That was something new too. But every time a girl got too close to me I'd shut everything off.

Like turn every tap off. No more Rene. I turned cold. I did that to almost all of them.

I used to see clueless and dejected looks from the girls that tried to caress my curls. I got enraged. I could never figure out why. I just slapped them away and said, "Please don't do that." But something deep inside me wished for the times that Nookomis, my grandmother, would caress my forehead and brush my hair back, like she did when I had a fever. She'd build a hammock, or rather, a blanket suspended by ropes at the ends in the room. Then she'd swing me to sleep.

Eventually, I started going to hairdressers; that sounded more gentle and classy. I'd have a few shots of whiskey before I'd let a hairdresser cut my hair. I hated barbers. But whiskey gave me courage to let a woman style my hair.

These days I don't need a drink. But, I still go to hair salons and let a coiffeuse style my hair. It has to have a fancy name. Barber, no. Never. But that's another peeling, I guess. All the abuse, you can't deny it. Plus, a hair salon had a better ring than barbershop.

Odjiishigi, Scar

Odjiish (cut from something); igi (heal).
A scar tells a historical story.

Restless

I had lots of jobs after I got out of Sheridan College, but none of them lasted long. My brother Ken had moved to Ottawa, and I moved there and got a job at the Office of Native Employment, Public Service Canada, as a graphic artist. I stayed for about two years, but I was homesick for the forest. I felt stifled by the four walls of the cubicle I had to sit in all day, and I remember thinking, *I don't want this kind of life.* There was no action. So one day I told my boss, "That's it. I'm going home." They tried to transfer me to the Museum of Man, but I only wanted to go home to fight forest fires. At least that way I would be outside.

I took the train to Nakina and from there went to Geraldton, saw my dad, and said, "I'd like to get on." He said, "Sure, let's sign you in!" It was easy to get a job in those days; just walk into any office and, "Hey—you're back!"

That firefighting job was with the Ministry of Natural Resources, and soon enough they offered me a position in the district office—a big building where my job was to make maps from aerial photographs. That was a steady job, all year round. I don't know how long I stayed there—maybe four months. I could have stayed there and made maps for all of northwestern Ontario, but I wanted to design things; I wanted to be creative. So I walked out of that one too.

Another time there was this guy from KC (Kimberly-Clark) who came to see me one day in Aroland. He knew I had graduated from Sheridan and wanted me to do some safety posters for the offices. I was going to draw things like power saws and these big tree farmers with bulldozers—you know, that kind of safety poster. But again, that was an office job. I also didn't want to work with KC cutting down the forests. I remember wondering why would I cut trees down and then plant them at the same time? I couldn't relate to that. *Values*—that's what the Ministry of Natural Resources always talked about. "We have to protect the timber. That's why we fight fires!" Private property, like those cabins that people have out there, like those fishing camps—"We've got to save that. That's called value!" I learned this in a fire suppression course or something. They were telling us, "Timber has a value. And so do those cabins. We protect them, and we protect the towns and cities!" So Kimberly Clark wanted me to cut those trees down, and the Ministry wanted me to save trees by planting and fighting fires.

Moving through all those jobs, I told myself that the restlessness was because I didn't like the jobs or I didn't want to be boxed in, but it was also because of the rage and depression. Nobody knew. I was cool, calm, and collected on the outside, and I kept getting offered more responsibility with every job. But on the inside I always felt, *I don't deserve this job.* At the same time, addictions took most of my energies—and working interfered with my drinking. Even having a relationship with anybody interfered. I looked at that as extra garbage, *I don't need it.* So I'd break off a relationship quickly, as soon as I felt someone was getting a bit too near.

Overall, my decision making just wasn't there. I had been set adrift, and I was only hoping things would turn out right. That's how I lived my life after residential school. I always had this voice in my head that said, *Rene, you're going to fuck up sooner or later.* Especially when something nice was happening, like marriage or a job. I always had this voice saying, *Rene, you're going to screw up, you're going to fuck up.* I believed this voice, and I did screw up. I would get drunk—that was the only decision I could make: *I'm going to get hammered today.*

I lived like this, moving around doing firefighting, tree planting, and other jobs until my late twenties when I made an attempt to live the life I thought was the proper one. I went back for retraining at Confederation College to take up electronics. My brother Ralph and I went together, promising each other, "Let's stay sober at least until

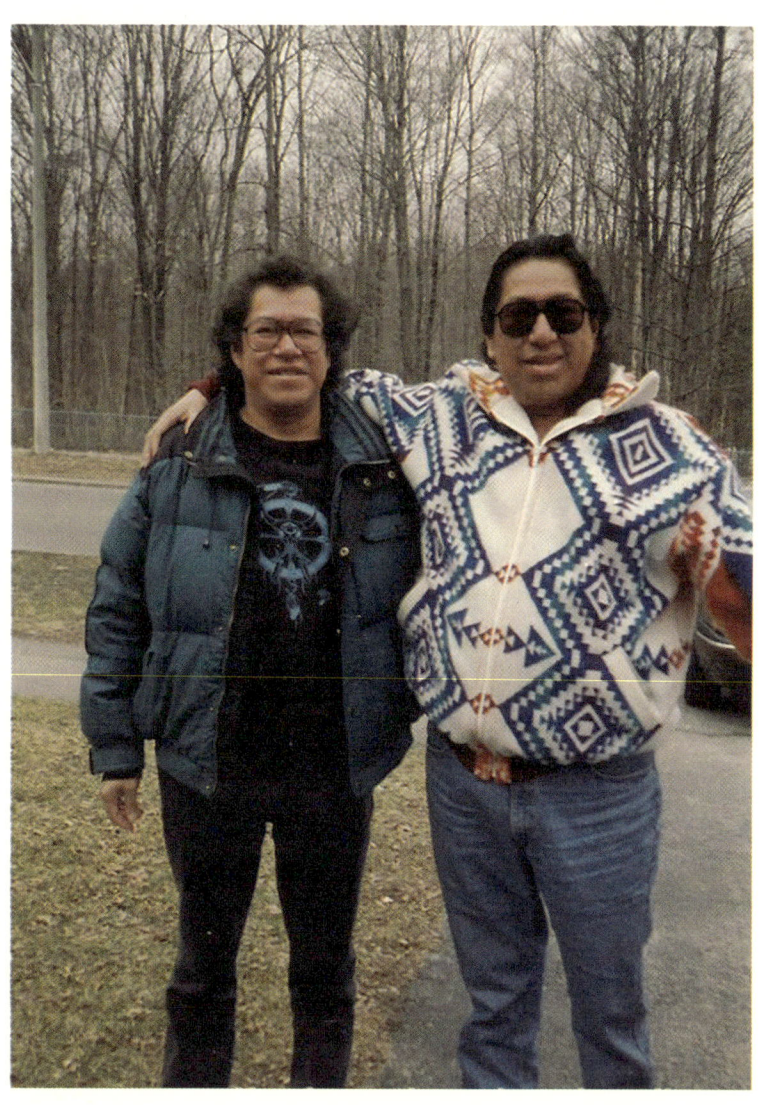

Rene Meshake and Ken Meshake, c. 1993. Photo by Joan Bruder.

we finish this program." We lived in a halfway house because we had to have some kind of institutional structure—we didn't know how to stay sober on our own. At least that house had no drunks in it.

When we graduated, Ralph moved and I started working for Canada Car doing wiring for the Toronto streetcars. I liked it at first but after a while it got boring because I was only soldering parts. Then I got married in 1978. I thought marriage, responsibility, and a steady job would make me stay sober. But I was quitting for someone else, not for Rene. I quit to finish my course at Confederation and then I quit for my wife and my stepsons, the house, the job, maintenance, groceries, providing—all the things I thought husbands should do.

It didn't work, and I ended up back to the lifestyle where the more money I got, the more cases of beer I could find. I'd be drunk and go to work—in those days I could drink all night and go to work the next day, no problem. I did that for about two years, and when they had a strike at Canada Car, I thought, *never mind, I'm not going back.* I couldn't do the lifestyle anymore anyhow, as I would be too hungover to work the next day. Some of my friends started going to Montreal to work at Bombardier because there was more money there. I didn't go because I didn't care for money; I just wanted to drink. I was right back to my old habits, and because of that I lost everything.

Stuck

All through my twenties I moved around a lot, back and forth—I was so restless all the time. I never stayed long with my dad and grandfather in Geraldton, maybe two weeks, and then I'd leave for Aroland or Nakina. I partied constantly. I had a lot of people to stay with, like my aunts, or I'd go with my cousin—we would get drunk in those days. That went on for several years: Geraldton, Thunder Bay, Aroland, and Ottawa and North Bay even, although I can't remember why I was there. It was that kind of world; drinking, partying, here there and everywhere. Wherever I hung my hat. Homeless.

Sooner or later I wanted to go other places. My marriage had not worked and around 1983 I thought, *I'll go to B.C. There's more action over there, more forest fires. And there's mountains—yes!* So I told my dad, "I'm going!" I left with only the clothes I was wearing and got on the train headed for B.C.

When I stepped off the train in Winnipeg I got held up admiring the station. I'd never seen anything like it—it looked so old and beautiful, and I was in awe of all the carvings. And that's where I met Johnny, an old friend from Thunder Bay.

"Tell me where the liquor store is!"—was the first thing I said. "Show me the ropes." So I stayed. I got stuck there.

In Winnipeg they had the projects; they had shelters, and there were welfare workers there to take your name down so you could get a room someplace. But once you got on this welfare you had to report any money that you made. It seemed to me that you couldn't save to get a better place. If you reported back and you had money saved they'd cut you off.

Through the welfare office I got a place with other drunks, and there were all sorts of people that I lived with. One time there was a guy in the house that started tying ropes all over the rooms, up and down the stairs. The landlord came over and said, "Hey, what are you doing?" They guy said, "The buffalos are coming this way!" Then I tried one of his medications—it was like a horse tranquilizer. When he gave it to me, he said, "Here, this will fix everything." But my head just felt so heavy, like, 5,000 pounds.

One day some crazy evangelist came to the house to save this guy. They prayed over his head and everything else. They said, "You're cleansed! You're cleansed!" After they left I could hear the showers running all night. That guy took showers nonstop to clean himself of sin, but he was hammered at the same time—that's those drugs he was taking; they were enough to stop your heart. Early the next morning I heard the landlord say, "Hey, where's all the hot water?" So I ran into people like that. I don't know to this day whether he's alive or not.

At one point I started looking for more action and I found a job as a roadie. I worked for a band that had a big bus and miles and miles of these cables. Big thick ones. I'd set the band up and then when I was done I worked security. That was the job. We got paid in drinks, but I didn't care.

Eventually I didn't work, and I was just stuck there in Winnipeg for the next three years. Drunk. It was a blur. No memory. Just party. Walk into a bar, stagger out and fall into another door and there's a bar again, back and forth. It was that kind of lifestyle.

Inendagos, Destiny

Inenda (will or thought); dagos (destined, I am).

It's amazing how Nookomis linked the mind with destiny. Whose mind? Inendagos describes how your destiny is divinely inspired.

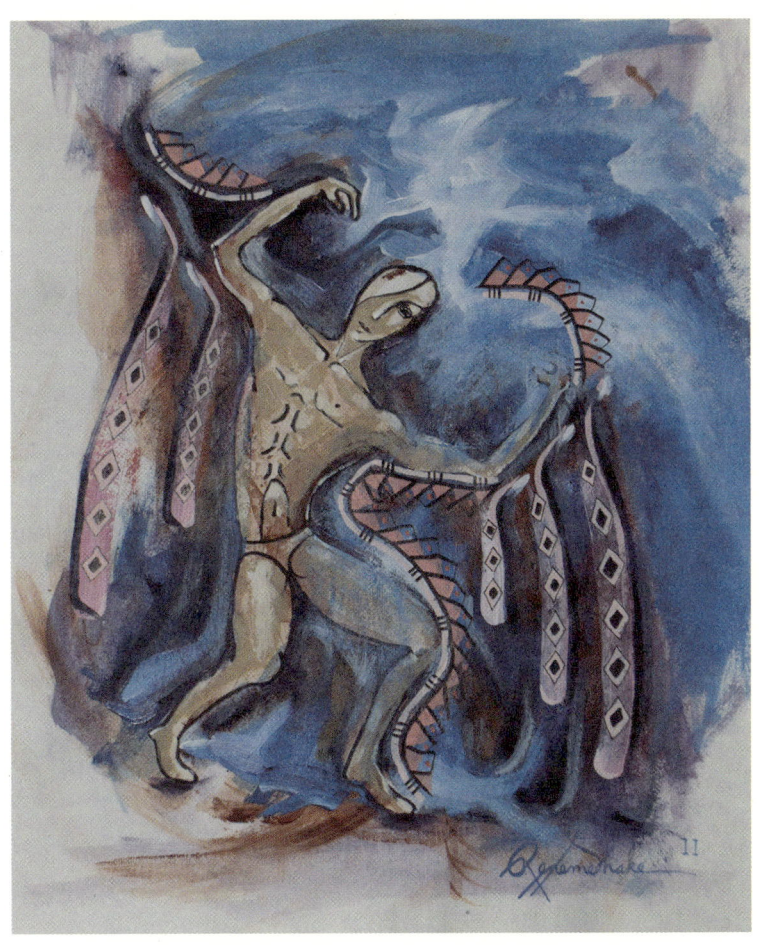

Nimiiwe, I Make People Dance, 2011, acrylic on paper, 33 x 43.2 cm.

Mangide'ewin, Courage

Mangi (enormous); de (heart); ea (make); win (state).

In harm's way, mangide'ewin is discovered. Fear gives you a larger heart than what you started with.

My Frigid Boxcar

Winds howl
and growl,
lashing the CN station.
Indoors the cast iron
parlour stove crackles
and sparkles.
I wiggle my toes
inside my shoes.
A distant train moans
and drones.
Her killing wheels plow
and race to disavow.
I am wakened
and straightened
by a strange, big hound
licking my face. I bound
up from my ice-covered sleep
to keep
warm, and spar
with death in my frigid boxcar.

Beyond Bi Ayaa

To Ken Meshake, 1950–2002

At the news of your death,
the world fell on its back.
I tightened my fists to the wreath,
trying to pull you back.
I ran to the beach and ran through the waves
past a dehydrating fish skeleton.
His scales held fast to shield themselves
against the basting brushes of the sun.
Flies mount, hone,
and embed their golden green bodies
on a white jawbone.
One like a flying ember decrees:
"Weshkad gipi maadjaa
Omaa gaye gondose
We beyond BI AYAA
September nights to stay
Roll back to the Meshake era,
when believing altogether
that life devours death beyond BI AYAA
My dear, dear brother."

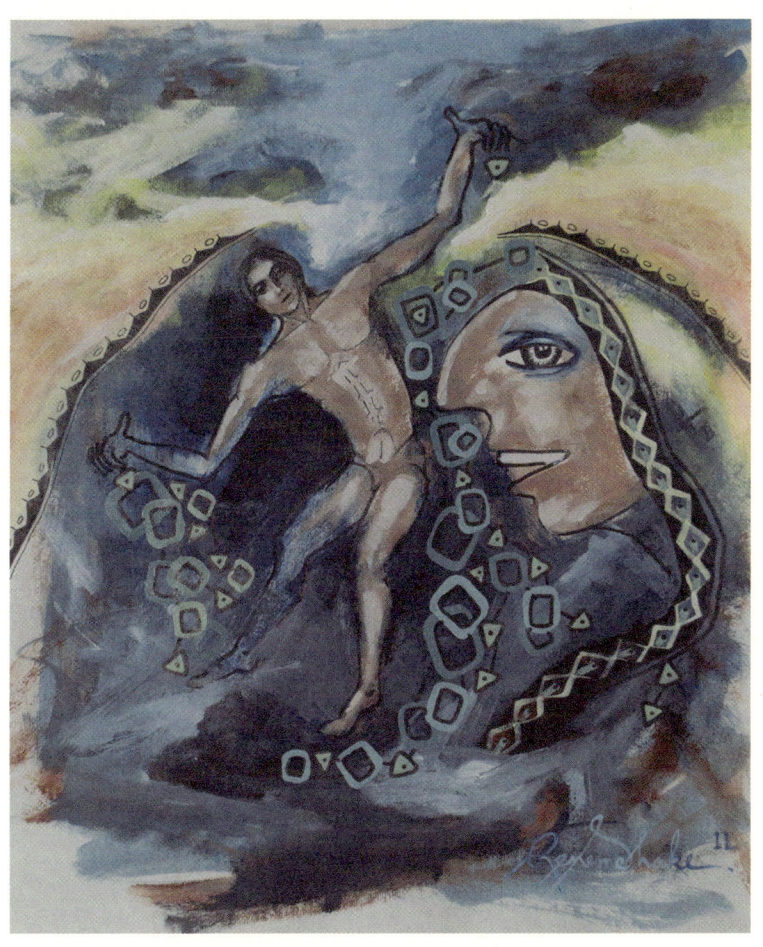

Songidee, Strong Heart, 2011, acrylic on paper, 35.6 x 43.2 cm.

Bathurst & Queen

While I was in Winnipeg my dad died and I went home to bury him in Aroland. That's when I made that resolution:

You know Dad, you're the last tie I have with this land. You're the only reason I kept coming back, but now there's nobody. So I'm never coming back here. Never, ever again. I'm going away, and I don't give a shit where I'm going.

My dad had left me a little bit of money, but I didn't want it. I told my brother Kenny, "You can have the estate. You can have it all. Where I'm going I don't need anything." But my brother did send some of that money. I knew I was going to get drunk with it, so why didn't he keep it? I was thinking, *he has a family, I don't.* But I ended up back in Winnipeg with money on me, and I partied. Got my friends together, got a hotel, and got really drunk.

The next morning I was down at the hotel reception talking to the clerk when I saw these two pilots walk by in their suits. I called out, "Hey guys, where are you going?" and they answered, "We're going to Toronto, non-stop!" I told them I was coming, and they said "You still have time. Go get your ticket."

I had money left over so I took a cab to the airport, still drunk. I made it onto the plane and drank more during the flight, and when I landed in Toronto a friend from Sheridan College picked me up. I stayed on his farm for a couple of days before going back into Toronto. I was planning on going to visit my brother in Ottawa next, but I soon forgot about Ottawa. I spent all my money and that was the start of six years of homeless life in Toronto.

I already knew some of the Anishinaabeg street people, like all those guys that used to hang out at Bathurst and Queen. I started partying with them and they told me, "You're one of us." That drunken feeling still gave me social closeness, plus they were drinking just like me. We had a gang. And on the street you form alliances, you get information about where to eat, where the shelters are, where everybody stays together. I think all the homeless are like that: we find acceptance with each other. You're like me; we're all equal, and respect is there. That's protection. Togetherness. Closeness.

I had always had trust issues with people because of the betrayal at Indian residential school, but I learned that I could trust my street friends. They earned it when I found out they would never betray me. The cops were always checking up on us first because we were Anishinaabeg. They were always around, trying to find out if we knew anything, but nobody ever said anything. You don't rat out on anyone, even if you witness something.

Living on the street was just like living on the trap line. I was used to the cold. And the tall buildings were like canyons, the streets were like rivers, the corners were where my traps were. One strange thing about winter homelessness is that when you enter a building or house you fall asleep because it is unbearably hot. I always wanted to go outside to feel alive. So I never felt the need to work. I found a way to live without money, without a roof over my head, and that's what made it hard to get off the street. Panhandling came easy to me, because I learned how to do spoken word and read people. I would tell stories, and if a guy was with a girl you always got more.

For shelter we'd find these places; abandoned houses, sheds—or we would build these little shelters under the Bathurst Street bridge. There were other people living with us too, like bag ladies. When we were in our sheds everyone had their own bed and we'd sing right through the night. People usually left us alone in the alleys along Queen Street, as long as we didn't set fire to anything.

I never needed welfare in Toronto because all my friends had welfare. My thinking was that if I was just going to spend it drinking, what was the point? I've got my buddy here, he's got his cheque, that guy has his cheque. But now they're all dead. Imagine that—because they were all so generous with their money. They're Anishinaabeg!

There were all these other groups, like the teenage homeless, with their spiked hair and neon colours. When I was panhandling I'd give all my small change—pennies, nickels, dimes—to the youth. Sometimes I had a lot of money and I'd invite them for a sandwich in one of those Queen Street greasy spoons. They didn't drink; they were more into drugs. That's their lifestyle. Each group had their own world in the city.

Sometimes there were these white people—a different crowd who just drove around partying in their car and being nice to everyone at Christmas. You could get in the car and drink with them, but I never did. My friend did. He was a black Indian and when they took him to a nice big party he said he was the only black face in the whole crowd!

There were also the "pensioners"—that's another group of people—and I spent more time with them. They'd invite you to sit with them. I'd sit with "Papa" all the time. He'd invite me to join him when he got his cheque.

One of our methods of staying warm on the really cold nights were the booze cans, which were open all night after the bars closed. All you needed was an entrance fee; you saved enough for that and your first beer. Once you were in, everybody drank and somebody always bought you beer. Sometimes that's where I stayed until dawn because you could also sleep there, and nobody bothered you. But it was only guys in those places; they didn't allow girls because girls meant trouble—fights happen. Also, those places were run by bikers, so if you started something they would bar you. You don't want to mess with those guys. You never steal beer or money. So the booze cans were always there, because if they got busted they would just open up another one down the street. There was lots of money in them and they were all over once you got to know people. There were crack houses too, but I only wanted to drink.

For clothing there were the donation bins; you would go and raid those things. I got a nice big fur coat one time—mink, I think it was. That was my sleeping blanket and it really kept me warm. I had a La-Z-Boy chair in an alley at Bathurst and Queen; I would snuggle inside my mink coat, push back my La-Z-Boy, and sleep there under the stars, just like on the trap line.

Sometimes we used social services like Anishinaabe Health Toronto, or sometimes I'd go to the detox and clean up. There were four or five detoxes where they would send you for a few days. They'd wash your clothes, and you could shower and wash your hair. You'd be cleaned up at least for one day, because on the street you have no time for it.

There used to be a lot of night buskers on Queen, but my favourite was Elvis. I would go and see him early in the morning after coming back from the booze can way in the east end of the city. There he was, somewhere around Adelaide, and just as the sun was coming up over the tall buildings it would shine a spotlight right on him, with his machine and his Elvis suit. A real Elvis, sometimes all in black. I would sit there with my bottle of wine and watch Elvis sing, and I'd clap for him and relax. Then the streetcar would roll by and come to a stop, and other people would clap and shout, "Hey, Elvis!" And Elvis would always respond, "Thank you ve-ry much." He was really into it.

Eventually he'd move on and I'd go too.

There were a lot of characters on the street. A lot of distractions; enough to keep the rage down. But when I was all alone—that's when I couldn't forget that terrible burning, deep inside.

In those years I couldn't see beyond Bathurst and Queen. My thinking was, *this is where I live, and this is where I'm going to die.* I was just waiting for death, and it wasn't coming soon enough. And then I started to see friends die. They'd go into hospital in a coma and never come back. Some died on the street in a coma—they just died— maybe it was violence or overdose. A dear friend of mine died choking on her own vomit. She grew old really quickly. Women seem to grow old faster. That's the homeless life, and it's not a good one.

Sometimes my own people, those that knew me, said, "Rene, you can paint and draw, why don't you just do a show and invite us all and we'll have wine when you do your opening?" Or sometimes I'd go in the bars and sketch something and soon enough I'd have a jug in front of me. I'd do a portrait or a fancy sketch and someone would like it and they'd take it away. So there were people that were interested in my drawings and wanted to do a show. There was even a recording studio that wanted me to do album covers. And I remember getting these matchbooks—there'd be phone numbers written inside. I'd look at them in the morning and think, *who is this?*—and I'd throw it away. Probably somebody who wanted a painting because there were a lot of people interested in my work. But I always thought, *you don't deserve this. You don't deserve an art show; you're a drunk.* I didn't want those fancy openings—that was too high class for me. Too up there, and I never felt comfortable in places like that. My thinking was that I belong here on the streets with my buddies, and I'm going to die on the streets.

Gishig,
Day

Gis (heat); shig (be).

The day gave us energy, the gift of work and creative activity. Have
we lost the meaning?

Institutionalization

I've been thinking about institutionalization. I got institutionalized by the church, the Indian day school, and the residential school. Then I took it to the next institution: jail. It's followed me all my life.

This was not the path intended for me as an Anishinaabe. I was raised by my grandmother and the matriarchs, and their job was to create a man; an independent man that goes out into the world to hunt, to provide, and to protect his family. They raised me to be an independent thinker who knows how to improvise, and they gave me the basics of how to live, how to get along. But then the schools took over from my grandmother.

The first thing they did in residential school was give me a number. I was #23, and with that I lost my humanity, my identity. Then they cropped my hair off and I no longer existed. I was no longer worthy. That is institutionalization.

I graduated from residential school as a non-entity, and when I went back to the rez, I had no sense of belonging. I didn't know how to integrate into the culture—the hunting, the fishing, the laughter, the storytelling, the music. It was like watching a movie; my mind would float above my body and I distantly observed my life unfolding; I was outside of myself. I guess that happened because I was always being told what to do, what to eat, what to wear, what to study, what to say, when to eat, where to eat, where to sit—I couldn't make decisions! That's why it had become comfortable to return to residential school after my summer visits home—because it was returning to an institution where I was told what to do, and it made no difference whether I was number 19, 20, or 21.

When I went to jail it was the same thing. I was told when to eat, when to change my clothes. Everything was done for me. And as someone coming from an institutionalized childhood, it felt very secure inside. Every time I got out of jail it was like the rug was being pulled out from under me. I found myself out on the street thinking, *what am I supposed to do?* I didn't know how to decide on anything. But you would have this probation officer that you reported to every week. The goal is to tell them you have a job and an apartment and you're doing well. But when that's gone and your probation is over, it's *uh-oh, who do I report to?* So you get in trouble again. I saw my brothers and sisters on the street and in the jails with the same problem. They needed permission or else they would get punished. And once probation was done, they'd be back in court again.

Those feelings and patterns went on well into my recovery. When I got married I would ask my wife things like, "What kind of shirt should I wear today?" I was always worried about pleasing. When Joan and I decided to buy a house it was also very difficult—I was so stressed out I broke out all over in a rash, thinking, *I'm buying a house; now what am I going to do?* I struggled over even seemingly small things, like the thermostat. I couldn't touch that thing; I had to ask Joan's permission. It's so institutionally ingrained: "Don't Touch! Don't Touch!" I think I couldn't take ownership—even though I "owned" the house, it was more like being a boarder in my own home. I couldn't do things, like move my desk to a more comfortable spot; in my head I would still hear, *If you did move things she might not like it and you're going to be punished.* Like Mother Superior telling me no, no, no, no.

Bonendamowin, Pardon

Bon or Boni (finishing, ceasing, stopping, or end of something); en-indi (think); win (state).

The Old Ones, the Anishinaabeg, were the closest to the truth when they said, "Bonendamowin." It means mutual pardon, forgiveness. It is not happening these days. We'd rather "beat the crap out of each other!"

The Tradition of Names

When I read about Betasamigishigweb (my great grandfather, born in 1834), it made me wonder what my name would have been when the land sat pristine and the lakes and rivers ran clear. When names were drawn from the land.

Betasamigishigweb. Beta (come); sami (walking); gishig (sky); web (draw water from). Betasamigishigweb comes as a sky walker who draws sacred water as he moves; the water of life that quenched the thirst for knowledge and medicines. Ishinikasowin (naming) like this reminded us only to serve, never to be served. To do otherwise would dishonour the core of your being. So in my forefathers' and grandmothers' generations, those traditional names ensured titles, reputations, characters, and office, as well as the success of our Anishinaabeg language, arts, and culture.

Imagine a name like Wakeiabanok, my great-grandmother, the one who married Betasamigishigweb. Wakei (circuitous); agan (morning); nok (woman). In times of need, this woman would have gathered medicines from afar, taking her journey longer than the direct way, with patience, perseverance, light. Imagine a name like Bidassamigishigok. Bidas (come); sami (walking); gishig (sky); gok (woman). In times of darkness, she would have been seen walking toward the stricken village, bringing a new sky of hope and revival. Then there was Iyabychewwage, a woman who makes double tracks wherever she walks—like moose do to confuse whoever is following them. Or Maysinagshkung, my uncle—a man who leaves a pattern or design behind him on the path he is walking on. All these names came through the visions of the Elders in ceremony, and they served our communities.

Nimishoomis, my paternal grandfather, told me that when his father was born, the Elders from our community gathered to give him a name. After much preparation, fasting, and prayers, all fell silent. Then one of the Elders spoke. He told the other Elders that he saw a damselfly hovering and descending from the sky. Mishakegishig: misha (descend); aki (earth); gishig (sky). "His name shall be Mishakegishig. He is going to hover and descend between the earth and sky for our people. He will be a teacher as his clan Mizay demands." But as time passed, Mishakegishig's name changed. His son, my grandfather, became Ambrose Meshake, a colonial name.

Who gave the right to the settlers to give us names, like the Meshake last name, which most of us bear to this day? Because of this intrusion, many of us have forgotten how each one of us should have a naming ceremony when we are born.

When I was young, the names of the elder men were spectacular, but the grandmothers' names were even more impressive. At that time I would only hear their traditional names if one of their friends or an older relative would tell me to go there; the adults could refer to that granny by name. When they were visiting with each other, I would sit and listen to them call each other by name too. But I couldn't say the grannies' names—the first time I tried, I was punished for that! Saying their names was considered very disrespectful.

That's where that manaten chimowin learning began. It means "handle with care." We learned that very, very early, about Elders, about grannies.

Now I can say with respect that my grandmother's name was Kitchi'gabwik. The name refers to "standing fast," and nothing could move her from where she stood. I ended up going to Indian day school, learning Catholicism, becoming an altar boy, learning to speak English—but Kitchi'gabwik continued to stand firm against all those things that were coming at us. Then there was her sister, Wemboma. Ma is "word," and her job was to arouse, to stir! By her words she could stir up people. She was a small woman, but she did all those things. There were other grannies, like De chi ka wik. De chi ka is when you look up, and there's a level place. She makes that. She makes the upper places level.

All those names that I couldn't repeat as a boy are now firmly in my head, and I look at how they commanded respect, obedience, a way of life. That's how I think our grannies governed our community—through their names. We understood the authority in those names, and we were trained from a young age to respect their role and position in the community.

So each culture had their own worldview, but the settler culture didn't respect ours, like when they started asking us to sign our names. Our culture was oral, no one read—and so they didn't know what they were signing. My granny didn't write her name, nor did Wemboma—they just made an "x," which we called aazhideyaatig. Aazhideyaatig is a cross, which meant death, so when they were signing their names, they were told to write their names with a symbol that we understood to mean death. It must have been hard to sign her name with an x—which means your name is dead, and then you are dealing with the Indian agent for those cheques.

I hope we can get that power of Ishinikasowin (naming) back, but it's hard if you take it out of the context of community. Our names meant something because people understood what the role was, and that's how you worked with each other. If you put a name out there in a public environment where you don't know anybody, don't have any community with them, before or after, it's kind of meaningless from the way we did it. Anyone can call themselves something like "Great Lightning Woman," but what does that mean? For us the name taught all about the respect in the relationship and in the grannies' case, about women, how they were governing the communities. So even when you have a name that sounds traditional, it doesn't bring that same awe in me as it did when I was a kid. That awe, rooted in the name, is what led to someone like my grandmother having authority in the community.

Today, most of us are dispossessed of the Anishinaabe names that might give us that honour; those titles, reputations, characters, and office. Instead, we've adopted European names, Christian names, soap opera names, and celebrity names. I have younger cousins back home that I see on Facebook, and they are having babies. I ask them, "Why are you giving your babies names that sound like crystals and chandeliers? Why not give them Anishinaabe names?" Then they say, "Well, give us names!"—and then I don't know what to do. Maybe I need fellow Elders to sit around and see the babies, and maybe one of us might have a vision—but I need land for that kind of vision to work, and to do that I would need to travel up north. There are still those ceremonies of giving a name, but then there is also becoming responsible for it.

I think about these losses—land, the treaties signed in x's, symbols, and meanings—but I also believe that the spirit of our traditional names is pervasive. It's the strength of the past that sustains me, and the spirit of names that propels me forward. And I am hopeful to see the youth beginning to reclaim our Anishinaabe languages and names, because these names can again draw from our lands to give inner strength, providing job descriptions and character to our youth. Then they can truly answer "Anish eshinikasi'ian?" and tell us about their names and their clans in a powerful way.

PART FOUR

Bimisi
Stories of Protection and Transition

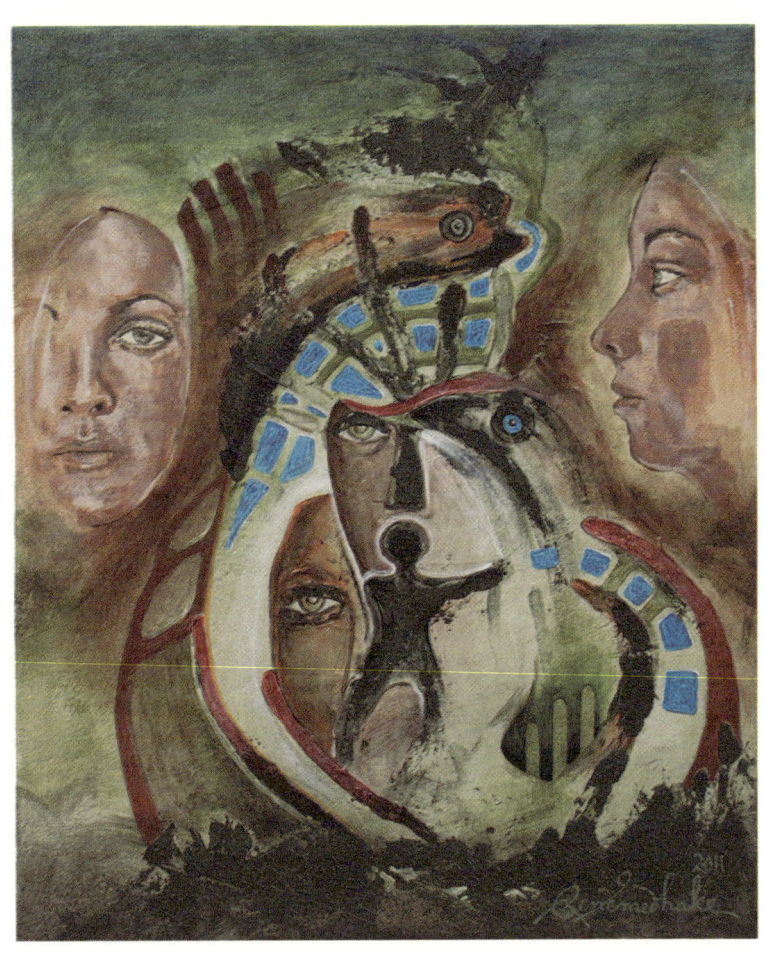

Bimisi, Eel, 2011, acrylic on canvas, 40.6 x 50.8 cm.

Bimisi

Bimisi, Eel. Bimi (passing through a place or places); si (eel).

Indigo dash Bimisi ishi bamashid naamiindip.

Weshkad megwa nibi gibi binagaming, Anishinaabeg Bimisi-bimide odagonigadowan biisikawaganing.

Midash, ishi miidjiwad ishpin manesiwadj midjim. Kawiin ni waabandasiin Bimisi gibideebison. Okishaadan ode'imaan nadji-monanion. Bimisi gi angowag. Wenish dash ge kishadang nind de'e?

Bimisi's name describes how the eel flies under water.

Long ago, in the time of clean waters, Anishinaabeg wore buck-skin jackets with fringes. The fringes were coated with bimisi oil and could prevent starvation.

If food was scarce, these fringes would be chewed. The oil provided nourishment.

I don't think that I'll ever see an eel-skin leather vest. This special vest was said to protect the heart. Bimisi has long vanished from the rivers. Who's going to protect my heart?

Tibikigissis,
Moon

Tibi (spin); ki (on); gissis (heat or energy).

This is a picture of the moon spinning in the heat of the sun. Light reflected on the face of the moon.

Radio In

I used to walk the logging roads in Aroland, carrying this 8 transistor radio. I loved to go into the bush and listen to it; I'd strut my stuff out there, thinking *nobody's watching anyway.* So I'd swagger to Elvis and Ricky Nelson, all the hits coming on.

I was fascinated with that little box of sound. How was it built? Did I just hear some rock'n'roll, some country; did I hear someone talking in this little thing? I wanted to know its secrets, and I resolved that I was going to learn how to make it work. That vision stuck in my head through high school, where I learned about math, science, mechanics, all the while still curious about the mysteries of this 8 transistor.

Years later, the opportunity came to attend Confederation College. I applied to study radio and television servicing, but I had to upgrade my high school subjects. My youngest brother Ralph and I competed against each other and we got these big marks—100%, 98%—never below. My marks in the college program were good too, and when I finished they said, "Rene, your marks are so great, we'd like to send you to Bombardier in Montreal; we want to put you into avionics." That would have been working on those big planes, wiring for the gears, the radio, all the electrical, lights. But I said, "I don't want to go to Montreal—I just wanted to learn how an 8 transistor radio works!"

The first thing I learned in my program was to put together an 8 transistor radio. We had tubes in those days; no integrated circuits, just a giant circuit board. I learned about frequencies, waves; how to tune it. I learned about calculating protons and electrons, positive and negative, how to slow the waves down. We have a hearing range, and I learned all about that. With all that science it wasn't a mystery anymore, and

I was having the time of my life learning it. When I graduated I knew how to fix radios, how to build them, and Canada Car hired me to do the wiring of the Toronto streetcars.

You no longer need transistors—there's thousands of them in this little chip. But I was happy with this radio schooling. It took me many years to get there. All that hard work to demystify the 8 transistor radio. That's education. It takes years.

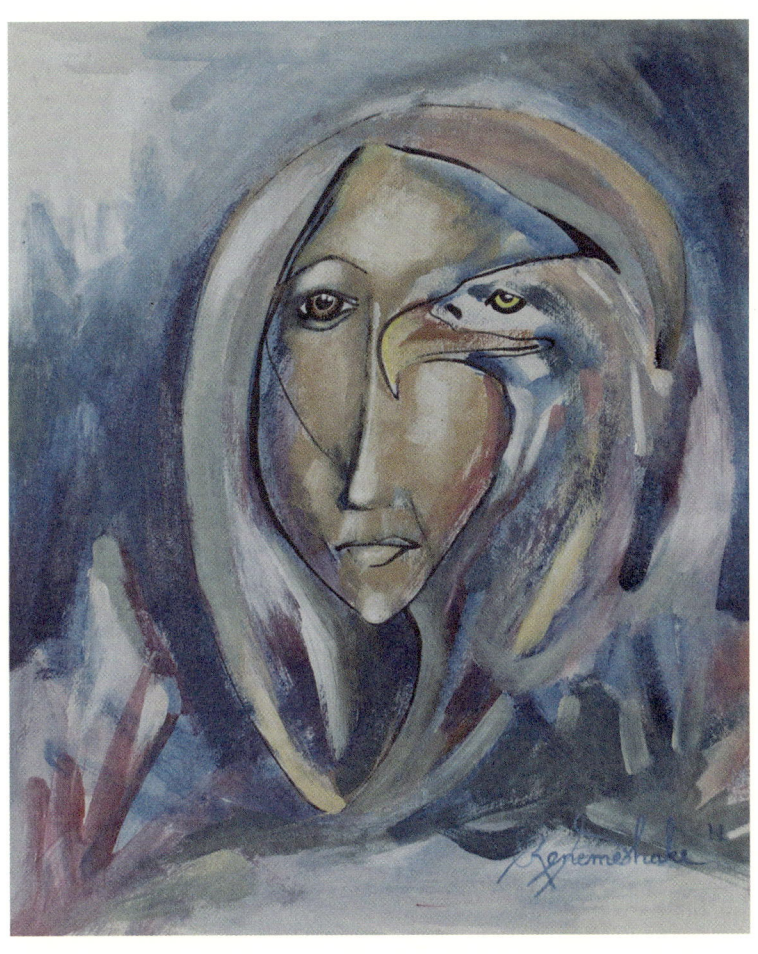

Tibishko, Two Simultaneous Events, 2011, acrylic on paper, 35.6 x 43.2 cm.

Giniw,
Golden Eagle

A lone eagle shot upwards
through a hole in the clouds.
"Disappear, don't you!"
cried the homeless Drunk,
shaking his fists to
defy how far he had sunk.
In the debris of rotting fruits,
the rats scurried, but came back
with new recruits
in the pack.
The Drunk knew that
even rats mourn their dead.
He heard wings pat
his shoulders and head.
He saw white buffaloes
floating over skyscrapers and plough
with slithering shadows
upon the checkered fields below.
"Now, we will live,
aware of the powers unspeakable
and thrive!"
he said to Giniw Golden Eagle.
Two eagles shot upwards
through a hole in the clouds.

Inside Out

When I was on the street in Toronto we used to pick up these things called tickets. They were for being drunk in public. We tried to get as many as we could—when cop cars came by we'd yell out, "Hey, write me out a ticket. You've got a quota to fill—come on, write me a ticket."

They'd bring out their little ticket book and write "intoxicated in a public place." There would be a fine attached—I don't know how much. Then when the weather got really cold we would say, "Well, let's go and cash in our tickets." Meanwhile, everyone in the whole district would be cashing in their tickets!

The way it worked was you would walk into the courtroom and say, "I've got about fifteen tickets on me and can't pay the fine." Then they would throw you in jail. That's working the system; that's how you got out of the cold. But I think too many of us were doing it— you had Anishinaabeg doing it, white drunks doing it, all the drunks doing it. Eventually the judges got wise and they didn't throw us inside anymore because the jails were already packed with serious criminals.

There's a lot of crazy things that happen when you're in jail. One time, my friend and I were in the Don Jail—I don't know why—like a lot of the episodes in my street years it is a blur. But I do remember the judge saying to the prosecutor, "Do you mean these two men were in jail for four days without ever coming to court? Get them out of here!" I was still in my blues, so I asked, "Can I get my clothes at least?" and they gave me twenty-four more hours. But the other guy, Luke, he went back to the street in his prison blues.

A couple of times I went to jail for protecting women—it's harder on women, living on the street. I remember one incident involving a good friend who was being abused. I just went over and talked to this guy who was abusing her, and I guess he got scared and told on me. Now I'm not endowed with muscles; I'm not a street fighter. But I ended up with an assault charge. He said he was sleeping on a park bench and I punched him out. I didn't even touch the guy, but I did time for that.

Another time I was in the Don Jail and became friends with the quarter man through studying. You can take courses inside, which is nice. I was taking mathematics; I don't know what he was taking. The quarter man is the cell boss. You've got to ask him permission for everything because he runs the whole cell block. So one day these younger guys were going at a big punching bag, making lots of noise when they hit it. The quarter man just walked over and took it down. He said, "I'm going to study, and I want everybody to be quiet." The whole cell block went quiet and we were able to study all the way to lunchtime—that's how much power he had.

When the quarter man left, he was always replaced. I guess some guys had been there so many times they just assumed that authority. There was even a quarter man in the infirmary, and that's often where I would end up, having told the guards, "I'm really sick here." In the infirmary they would shoot you full of drugs, and there were beds and doctors. I would tell the doctor, "I've been drinking too much on the street." You never wanted to go cold turkey because you'd get withdrawals that involved bouncing and shaking and sweating and everything else. So I'd say to the guard, "I need the infirmary; I can't handle this."

That's the story about being inside or outside; it didn't matter to me. It was just a way of life. I didn't mind the jails because I was so institutionalized from the residential schooling. In jail, they told me when to change my clothes, when to eat, when to get up and when to go to sleep. You got four meals a day. Everything was structured. And when I got out, sometimes I didn't know what to do.

But there were rules in both places. On the inside, you abide by them and you get out alive. There were checks and balances, and we'd police each other. We were all against the guards because nobody trusted them. The quarter man was the one who had respect; he was tougher than you, and he had earned it. He kept the peace and all the guards knew it. The street was similar; we had our own police and we knew the rules, but it was more violent there.

It's a cycle. You're in and out. It's just like those little hamsters on their treadmills. You're running but going nowhere. And that's the only world you know.

Apinimowin, Loyalty

Ape (depend on); nimo (confident); win (state).

Loyalty among the Anishinaabeg is the highest value. I can see why dependability was valued in times of famine or disease in the old days!

Waginak,
Rib of a Canoe

Wagi (bend); na or nak (wood).

The rib is not an inanimate object. Wagina describes a person bending and holding the rib bent in the canoe. The living birchbark carries you across the lake.

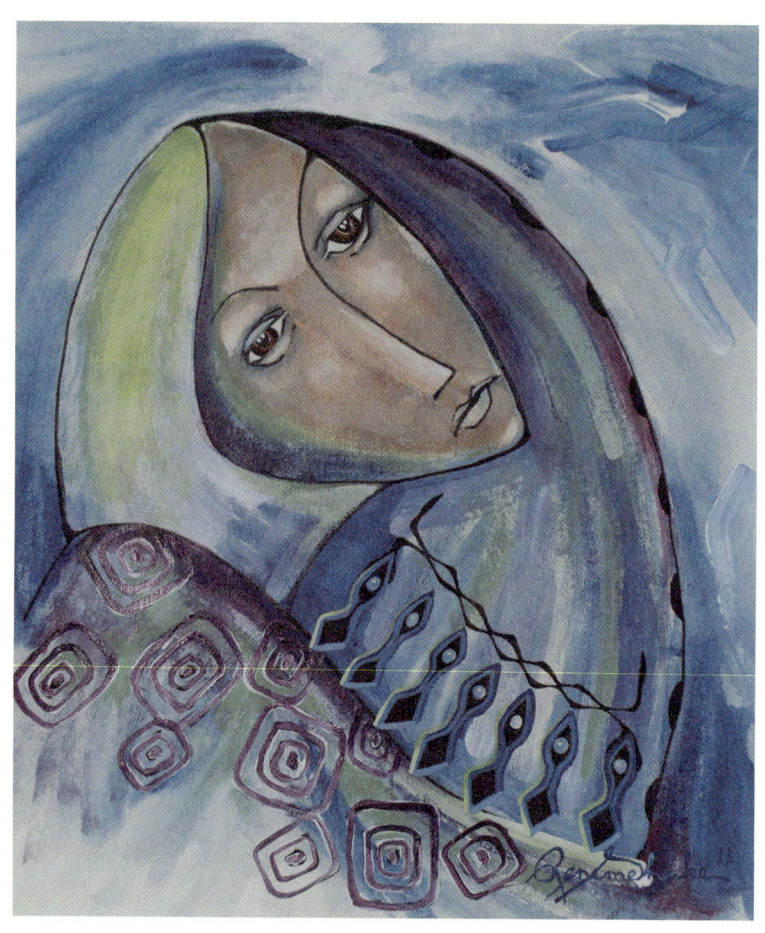

Pisindam, Listen, 2011, acrylic on paper, 35.6 x 43.2 cm.

Slingshot

Slingshots were prized items when I was a kid. We built them out of old tires, some of which had dead rubber, so you had to find rubber that was still elastic. We would look for tires at the dump, and you were a rich kid when you found good ones. Some kids had large pieces of rubber, and I had rolls of it. So I was very rich, and I made the best slingshot crutches.

I remember one time that there were these Metis boys visiting. They were all teenagers, and Richard was the one I admired the most. We never really hung around with these guys—as a kid you're not in the club yet. They used to shovel off the lake to play hockey at Longlac. They weren't drinking much then; there was a lot of sports— hunting and fishing.

On that day Richard had this slingshot and I couldn't stop looking at it because of the carving on the crutch. I kept handling his slingshot, and then I'd give it back to him.

In the evening, just as they were getting in their pickup, Richard said, "Rene, come here." Then he handed me that slingshot. I just adored that guy. He was like a god. I even combed my hair like him! And then he said I could have his slingshot. I almost cried I was so happy.

After that I started making other crutches, and I tried to imitate his carving in the curves and notches. The more I copied his style, the more I developed my own, and my crutches became really ornate too. When I finally made one fully my own—that's when I became Rene instead of trying to be Richard. Then it was my turn to pass this down to my younger cousins that hadn't known even how to draw a knife.

That's how I remember Richard. He didn't do much—just gave me the slingshot, but it taught me a lot. Out of that I learned how to hunt. I went deeper and deeper into the woods to hunt partridges.

I worry that many of our young people don't have those tools available. Do they have teachers they observe? What if they see empty cases of beer—beer bottles on, or under the table, you know, whisky bottles, and vodka bottles. If that's all they see—what kind of tool is that? That slingshot, it was a great example of what tools we leave for others.

I was lucky, too, because I had my uncle Peter (Biidan); he was the guy that had all the tools for making canoes, and he would leave them around so I could eventually pick them up. And when I was about ten years old, Biidan finally asked me to go hunting with him. That was showing a respect for me, and I felt like, "Whoa, I'm a big guy now!"—even though I could barely keep up with him. But he trampled down the twigs and everything to make a path for me to follow him through the bush.

Seeing all that was very powerful imagery of what I could become, setting the pathway to be an older cousin or an uncle to somebody else someday.

Sweater No. 23

Opening a page of my copy of the Old Timers' hockey game,
I saw where Eddie Shack, the hockey legend, had signed his name.
It swept me back to the fact that
he wore sweater No. 23
on his way to a Stanley Cup win.
I, a rookie, in the Indian residential school
wore sweater No. 23.
The name the staff had given me
instead of calling me
by my real name.
Eddie got penalty calls for pushing,
shoving and fighting in the NHL.
I'd be elbowed at the centre ice at school.
No penalty calls. ·
Missionaries: 9, Ojibwe: 0.
Each "Hockey Night in Canada" on TV,
I'd walk from the dressing room
of my mind to watch *Nagaji,*
the on-ice stratagems of my
favourite hockey star.
With a standing ovation,
I'd reach around the back of my neck
and stretch my shirt collar to see
No. 23 on the label.
Yes!
"Clear the Track Shack"

rallied the fans,
they were the Toronto Maple Leafs!
Eddie picked me up as well.
I'd lost track of "The Entertainer"
until he signed his name
on the page of my Old Timer's hockey game program.
Eddie, the Veteran.
I, the Survivor.

Namekwan,
Glue

Name (sturgeon); kwan (stick on).

Glue is made from sturgeon and it's used as an adhesive in paint pigments. Think Agawa Canyon pictographs. Anishinaabe artists knew chemistry!

Improvisation

The government put us on reserves to keep us in one place, and so they built reserve housing. This was different than living in a tent, which was very mobile. But in my early years, every now and then my grandmother would pull me out of Indian day school and we would leave the reserve. Nookomis would put up that tent anywhere in her homeland. We'd live in it maybe a week or two and then she would move it to the side—that way we didn't kill everything underneath. And so, along with the tent, some of my earliest schooling was mobile. But after a few years of Indian day school I was taken to residential school and then I got stuck in one place.

The residential school was very inflexible—everything was regulated. We had a time to get up, a time to do homework—and it had to work like a clock. But how could a person live in the bush with such a regimen? What if you're out there fishing and all of a sudden you need to camp? You need to know how to improvise.

I'll tell you a story about my cousin Howard and me. Howard didn't go to Indian residential school, although I'm not sure how he escaped it. But while I was at the residential school he was at home living on the trap lines with my dad and my uncles. He was trained how to live in harmony with the land and he knew the land, along with the animals.

One time I was home visiting with Howard; we were far out on the river when somehow our motor broke down and we lost all power. But we had just shot a couple of ducks, so what Howard did was butcher the duck and pull out the esophagus. I realized then that our gas line was broken, and he needed something to connect the two lines where

144

it had broken. Once he had the esophagus in place, the gas flowed through it and got us home.

I was so amazed—how did he come up with that? That's improvisation. I wouldn't know what to do in that situation; I wasn't brought up enough with my dad and uncles, and I didn't know ducks. All that was taken from me when I went into the institution.

Ishinashawagan, Messenger

Ishi (be); nasha (name dispatch); awa (that or this); gan (means).

The messenger or story that Ishinashawagan delivered depended on his or her name. Ishinashawagan's name is an instrument used to shape and form community.

Bebapinisidj

Mindamoye—that's the elder women. Then there's mindamoke-meshi—he was like a court jester. He would imitate these old ladies. I guess sometimes you needed some relief from these elder matriarchs. So he'd imitate how they walked—he was permitted to do this. They could also make masks out of birchbark. But the matriarchs were never offended. They just laughed.

The mindamokemeshi knew the backgrounds of the Elders, the things they said, and the sound of their voices—everything was repeated. He was a historian, too—he'd have to remember the history of things that happened. That was his job. My grandmother would have seen this done. When my granny saw the monkeys in my comic books she mentioned this word.

There are other words for that jester that had the job to imitate both the old ladies and the old men: bebapinisid, or bebapinisidj, or neta-bebapinisid. I tried it myself once. I remember there were three grandmothers and we had gone out blueberry picking. One evening they were telling stories, and I started dancing. "This is how you dance, Grandmother." I was the bebapinisid, and they laughed. Because I was living with my grandmother I knew every nuance she had of acting and talking. It was also educating me to be a performer. That's the first glimpse I had that I like to act.

Anybody could take on that role of bebapinisid, but you've got to be really good, and you had to really know the person. You're not mocking them; that would be disrespectful. There's a light side, but it can become a dark side if someone isn't good. So I wasn't making fun of my grandmother; I was just becoming her for about ten minutes, and the Elders around her had to really believe that's how she acts. You don't want to get up there as a young guy with no talent and have Nookomis say, "No, that's not me, you're making fun of me."

I guess that was a way to know if you were observing, if you were listening or paying attention. It was like a test, to see how well you know the story. I did it in the form of dance, making drum noises to tell some kind of story about a bear and how my granny would act. That is bebapinisid.

There was an act I saw a few years ago about these two Cree grandmothers, and it made people laugh. When those actors played grandmother with her kerchief on you believed them. They were not making fun of anyone. That is bebapinisid. So it still happens. But we could still use more theatre on the rez.

Dodem,
Clan

Dodem (clan); dodamowin (action or commitment).

The Anishinaabeg nation has a dodem system to confront what lurks beneath and arrive at the other side changed! Life can involve suffering. There will always be chaos as well as order in our lives. It is our dodamowin (action or commitment) to renew the balance between the two with ceremonies. Now that's a life worth living!

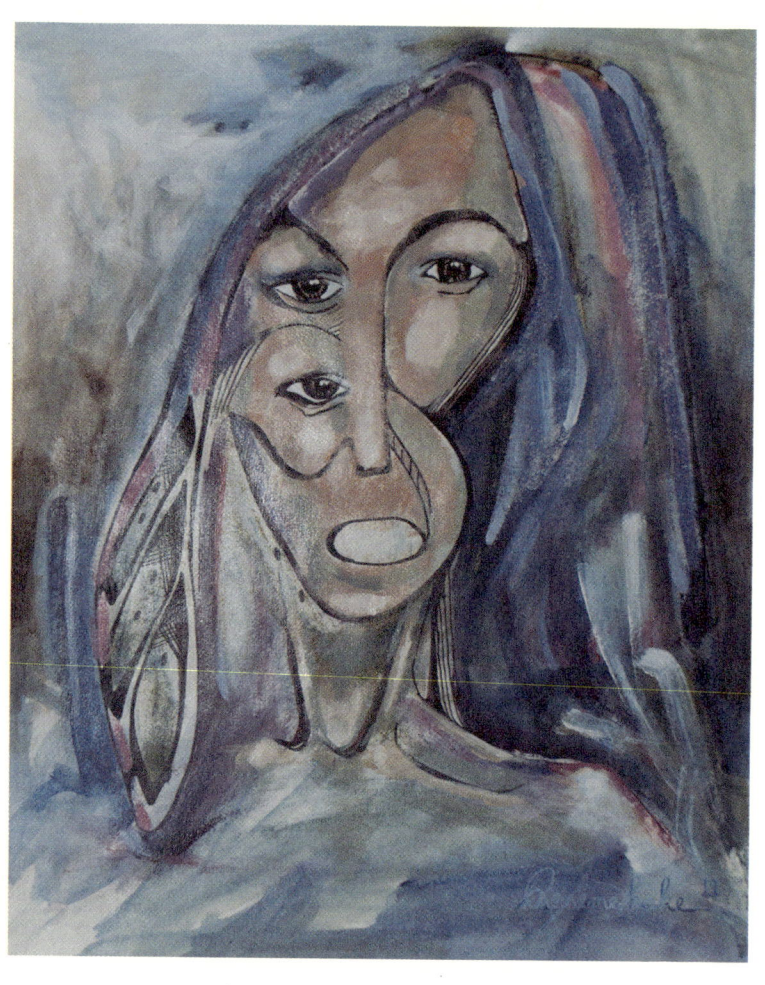

Inawendiwin, Relationship, 2011, acrylic on paper, 33 x 43.2 cm.

Raging Fires

When I left residential school I went back to Aroland, back to the rez, but I could never, never fit in. I felt so isolated; the closeness and intimacy I had always felt with my cousins wasn't there any more. So I started battling this depression that would last for weeks and weeks. There was an inner rage eating me up—it would gnaw at me. I kept wanting to go somewhere else, and the only comfort I found was in taking long walks in the forest.

During my teens I had found that the trap line took away some of the rage and depression. From November to May I only wanted to be out there with my dad or my uncles because the forest and the rivers and lakes would be all around me, and I could take long walks on the ice. I learned to cook because I didn't want to trap. I would make tea and coffee on the shoreline while my uncles were out looking for beaver lodges. They'd come back around evening and I'd have a meal ready for them. The days were very short, so we'd have to go back to our base camp where our aunts were waiting, and we'd have a nice supper. That was the routine. But I couldn't be there all the time.

Once I was home for good it wasn't long before I discovered alcohol. It was on a summer night at one of my uncle's parties and I think it was gin and 7-up. We were having a great time; my uncle was playing his harmonica or guitar and there was some record player blasting away and I was just dancing. I suddenly felt more at home, more alive. I wanted more of that feeling, to feel that much life, to feel that much spirit. I could talk, I could dance, I could laugh with my aunts and uncles. I wanted this closeness, this community feeling all the time, and alcohol seemed to have done it for me. I finally felt free from depression and rage.

I started drinking heavily from that point on, and there was only one other thing that took away my rage and depression: fighting forest fires. It was as if the more dangerous the fire was—like if there were crown fires over my head and the oxygen was sucked out of the air— the more alive I felt. I liked the smoke, the smells, and I liked when everything was moving and raging around me.

Firefighting had been my first job and I did it all the way up into my thirties. My dad worked in firefighting and when I was sixteen he told the chief forest ranger in Nakina, "Hire him, but you've got to watch him, make him stay in the camp." So at first I was a bull cook in the kitchen. I washed dishes, kept the fire going. Louis, the cook, was my uncle; if he needed water I'd get him water and I got wood to keep the fire going. But it was so boring. Eventually I started to follow some guys into the bush and then began my first experiences actually fighting the fires. I became my dad's clerk and pump man. The best pump man there ever was.

They did nozzle crew competitions during this period, five of us to a team. I got to be very good on pumps; I could start that thing in two minutes. What the nozzle man did was try to knock down these targets with water. Our main competitors were Kenora and Sioux Lookout—those big Indians up there. Kenora especially had big guys, oh man they were built. But we were fast. And we practised and practised. One thing we got tired of, though, was getting these Zippo lighters as prizes. My friend Emmett kept complaining, "Geez... another Zippo! Can't they think of something different?" Five Zippo lighters—that's for winning. As you advance you get a Zippo lighter. At least I used to smoke in those days. And then they'd put us up in these nice hotels in Thunder Bay, with big dinners and all you can drink, of course. There would be a big party and I would drink with the MNR staff. I worked for years fighting fires on standby—that's where we waited for fire reports—"Who's going out first?" We were the crew from Geraldton: there were five guys with my father. "Are we going to get an army chopper or a commercial one?" I didn't like commercial choppers because the commercial pilots didn't land close to the fire; they wanted to land in airports. I guess they were scared. But these army choppers—those guys land anywhere! They can put you down close to the fire—I guess they're trained for that.

The last firefighting job I was involved in was building heliports. There was this guy from Gull Bay and he could handle power saws. So we got stuck making heliports all over so choppers could land near the fires. They would drop us in the bush with a power saw and an axe. Those pilots loved us—especially the commercial guys who wanted a big wide field to land in. We'd build it so a 747 could land there! And because the pilots loved us, we got stuck doing this job. Sometimes we made too much money and they forced an R&R on us. I would go to Thunder Bay to spend it all—I always gave lots of tips. Then we'd fly back to the base and start all over again.

So that's what it was; the bigger the fire, the more alive I felt. I had to stay sober to fight the fire, but in the end the rage was still there when I came out of the forest and I would get depressed and start drinking again. It was this back and forth, running all the time.

Diamond Raindrops

Rainwater cleaves
to the fallen maple leaves
on my patio.
But where are you?
Rain merchants of the sky
dump diamonds
on my deck,
each a sunny fleck.
Stones glazed by
the downpour
come alive
with a drumming drive.
The wind taps more
on the patio door
giving me a clue
that
—it is you.

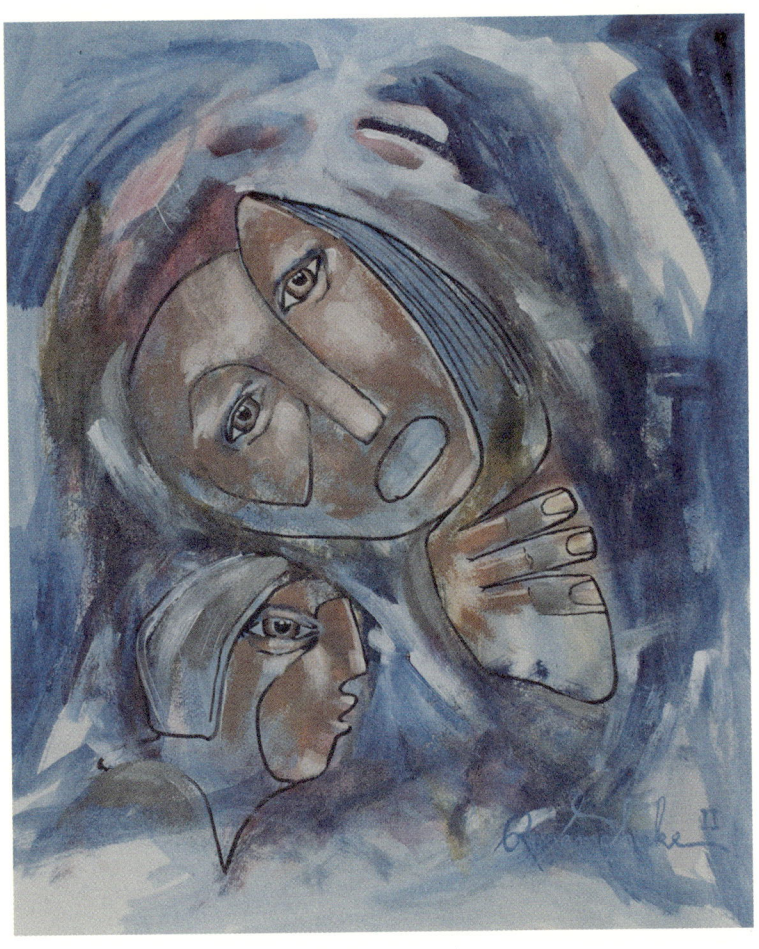

Widjiwagan, Friend, 2011, acrylic on paper, 35.6 x 43.2 cm.

Mamaasikaa, Movement

Mamaasi (to move out, in, or about); asikaa (from a certain direction).

To Aunt Emily

(1936–2015)

Oh! The night of my aunt be true,
I sit in my sorrow to weep
in the dark missing you,
watching you sleep.
Awake in the arms
of the Eternal Day, Emily.
Breathing anew rearms
your hands to pray.
Set fires to the oak.
Let my grief dissolve
in the rising smoke
with abiding resolve.
Minawa apii farewells we traded.
Since then I've raced
to gaze upon the makizinan you made.
Babiichii no more I haste.
Go! With your wings unfurled
upon the golden flowers
of your new floral world
and powers.
Gagiichii
I can see you
Makizinikeh under the Eternal Day
—It's . . . just . . . like . . . you!

Memegwessi

Memegwessi. They're the "wee" people. The wee nation or tribe.

Our Memegwessi live by the riverbanks and marshes. Always by the water—it's their mode of travel, I guess. I've heard even my older cousins say that they used to meet these guys when they were in their canoes and they looked like ajijaakons. That's a sandhill crane. They're that size. And when I met the ones in Ireland, they were the same size.

When Joan and I were in Ireland in 2017 we took a train ride out of Dublin, and at the end of this railroad line is Howth, right on the Irish Sea. I had been talking to this lady on the train and she mentioned this island that you can go to by boat from Howth. I thought it would be a big ferry like the Chi-Chi-Man in Tobermory, you know?

We ended up on the docks and saw this guy selling tickets for ten euros. I walked up to him, saw this big boat, the size of my house, and thought, *Oh, I'm going to go for a nice, nice ride.* I told Joan, "Let's get on," and we followed him, but we ended up in the smallest boat—the size of a fishing boat we would use up north! And we saw this huge American guy—he steps into our little boat and says, "I thought we were getting on a big ship!" He's not even dressed to go out there, just a t-shirt, and shorts, and stuff.

We got out and the waves were big ones. I said, "YAH!" every time a wave came along; that little boat was built to handle sea waves. I was standing there going up and down, just like a roller coaster. I was so excited, but everybody else sat in their seats, not saying anything.

As we got nearer to this island I looked up at the cliffs and I saw this face. You know, she looked like this lady—Lady Lavery as Kathleen Ni

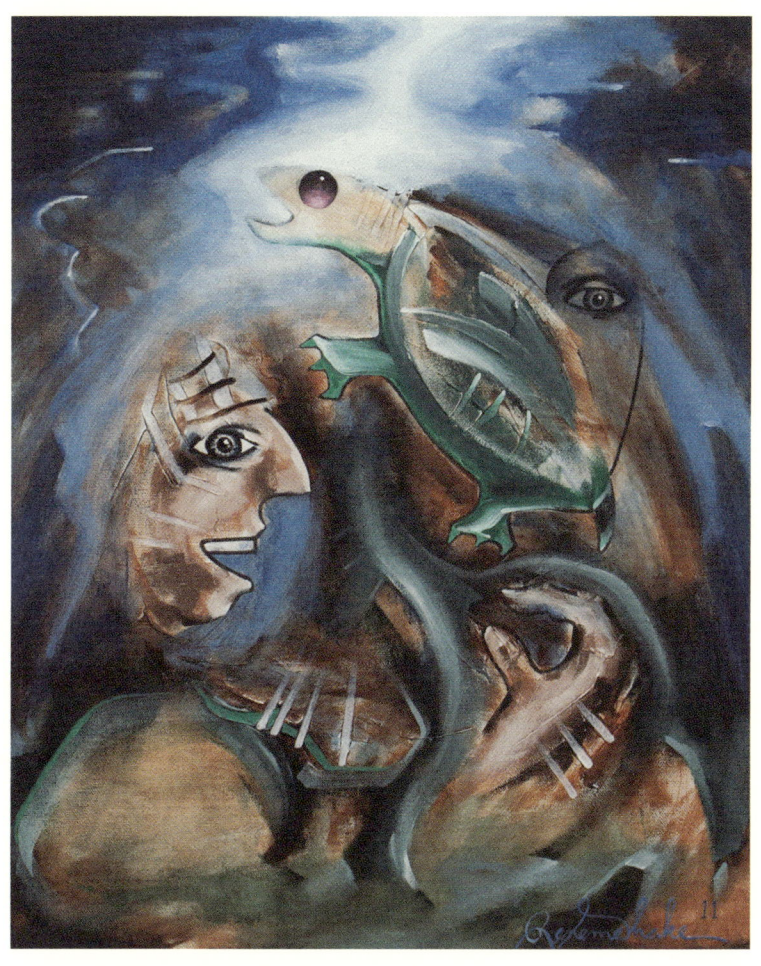

Miskwadessi, Turtle, 2011, acrylic on canvas, 40.6 x 50.8 cm.

Houlihan. Joan and I saw the original painting of her at the National Gallery in Dublin and that's where I fell in love with her. They had told us the story of this woman, who was also on the Irish money. And then I saw her on this island—I think it was her; I don't know. Anyways, after she disappeared and we rounded this island, it got rougher and rougher. I saw a movement on the cliffs and I thought *it can't be*—my head is saying, *it can't be those guys.* I couldn't believe it—nobody was looking.

But yeah, that was them. Little people. They stopped whatever they were doing and stood up. Every single one of them stopped to look at me. You know when you're busy doing something and then you stop and look?—that's what they all did. It happened just for five or ten seconds, like a flash. And then the seagulls came and started to move and kind of took over. They kind of blended in with the seagulls. But as we moved further I started to see these faces on the rocks. They're all just faces but they're still looking at us, you know? Similar to the memegwessi, but they were in the rocks. That's all I saw, and then we came back.

Then they weren't finished with me, these memegwessi. When we got to the airport, we couldn't find our passports. They were gone. We rummaged through Joan's luggage and couldn't find them; panic was starting to set in. Then I went into my bag and there they were. So memegwessi had something to do with this. I think they didn't want to let me go.

PART FIVE

Miskwadesshimo
Stories of Recovery

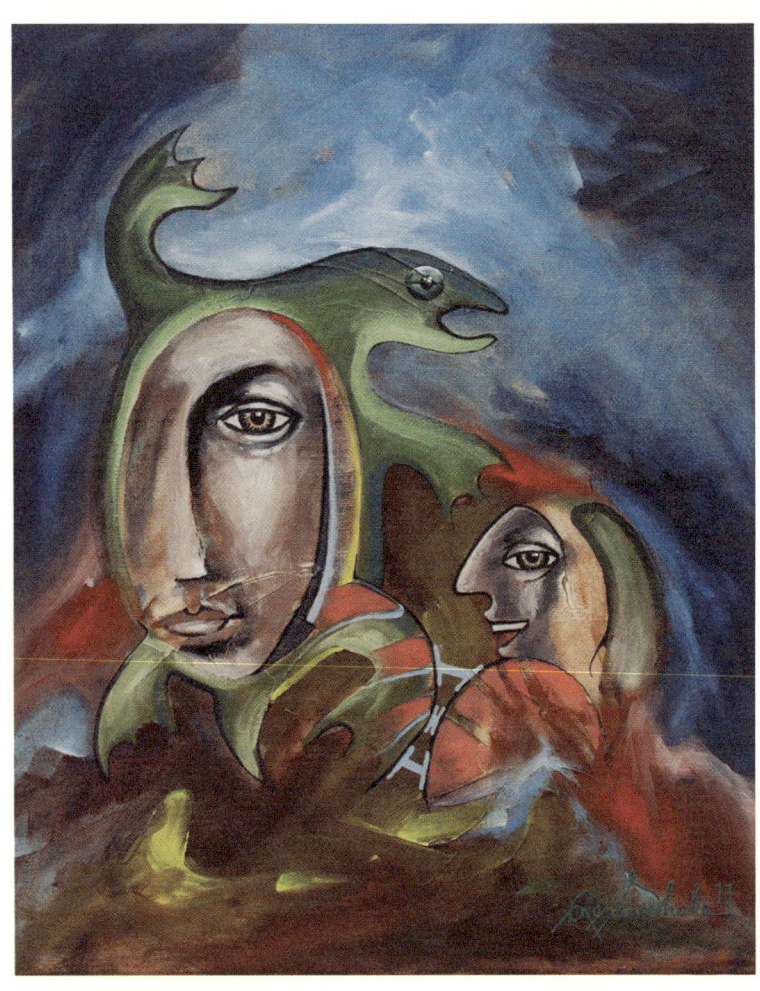

Miskwadesshimo, 2011, acrylic on canvas, 40.6 x 50.8 cm.

Miskwadesshimo

Miskwadesshimo, Turtle Dance. Miskwa (blood or red); des (shell being); shimo (dance).

A dancing Blood Being.

Madoodiswan ishkweia.

Madoodoowasiniig indigo miskwadessiig ishinaagossiwag imandi ishkwakodeng.

Pipigwen ikidowag pagidin miskwadessi chi aniimidj. Midash, miskwadessi neta-nimid ingi masinibi iwa mi eta ji nondawad ishpin waasseiadisian.

The Sweat Lodge was over.

I studied the black rocks (Grandfathers) in the ashes of the firepit. They looked like dancing turtles.

I could hear them telling me to play the flute and make the turtle dance. That night, I went to my studio to paint the turtle dancing to the music only your spiritual ears can hear!

Medicine Circle

When I was in Winnipeg I met this Elder named Stan Fontaine. I had heard about Elders, and I thought, *I'm going to check this out.* Stan had a lodge, and all the Anishinaabe from the streets went there. I remember him telling us about his drunken days, when he thought everybody else was crazy. I heard that and thought, *Hey, that's what I feel like. Everybody else is crazy—I'm sane, I'm okay.* That was the excuse: *I'm okay . . .*

Then he started talking about what he called the medicine circle. He told us there were four directions, and the first direction is kindness. He talked about sweetgrass and the grass that we walk on every day. Wherever there's grass, it speaks of kindness. It's the way you walk.

The second one is the tree, standing straight and tall. That speaks to the Anishinaabeg to be honest with themselves and others. That's the way it is. "Oyukshga." I remember thinking to myself, *Wow—this is good stuff.*

Next comes sharing. "You see all the animals around us? Moose, wolves, and all the creatures on earth remind us about sharing," he said. With the way that he talked, he drew me right in. He was a magical, spiritual person. I remember thinking, *That's the most spiritual person I've ever met. Just like my grandmother . . . Yeah!*

The last one he talked about was the mountains. Bedrock—really hard rock, and that's strength. That's where we get our strength from, to remind us about faith, hope, love.

After he explained the wheel, I remember his saying, "That's not all. Then there's the body. You carry the law in your own body. Your hair, that's like the grass. Kindness. There's a tree inside you, and that's your backbone. That's another law; your ribs remind you of a tree inside you. That's honesty—that's a human. Then the animal in you—that's the pubic area, the hair. That's the animal, the sharing. And I'll tell you something, too, you see a woman's breasts—they are kind of like mountains. That's strength."

I walked away for the first time feeling something about being Anishinaabe. Because all that time since residential school I had been denying myself being Anishinaabe. I hated me. But after this description of the law, the spirituality of each individual on earth, I felt, *Oh man, there's a law inside me. I'm worth something.* That was a powerful teaching and it really impressed me. I walked away and somewhere in my brain's hard drive that thing stuck there. He put it there. He gave me that. And when I went into rehab at Pedahbun Lodge, it came back to me.

Biidwewidam, Hearing

Biid (come); we (voice); widam (he or she).

Imagine sitting still in the forest alone and you hear someone's voice becoming clearer as he/she comes near you.

Eshpadinaa

I'm on a fast. I'm fasting from alcohol—it's my lifetime job; a vision quest. I've had mentors come my way, students and others who teach me things. But the ceremony of language is also so important in all of this. Even the name and the place where you start your healing journey is part of that ceremony. For me it happened at Spadina and Dundas.

Eshpadinaa: Spadina. White people say Spa–dye–na. We say Shba'–dinaa.

Eshpadinaa means rising hills. Eshpa means it has these terraces and then terraces and terraces. Dinaa means up there, the top of the mountain. Mountaintop is eshpadinaa. And that street in Toronto goes uphill all the way, you know?—as you go north.

When I was homeless and living under the Bathurst Street Bridge in Toronto, I used to pass this street called Spadina all the time. And when my friend Bobby died I buried him on one of those eshpadinaa in Toronto. Bobby was my best friend; we'd hung out together drunk and homeless in the city parks, alleyways, and streets. Then he fell into a coma and never came back. I don't know where the graveyard is now, but it's on one of those hills.

"I bury my past with you, Bob," I told him, standing on the eshpadinaa. And instead of pouring wine on the ground I sprinkled sand on his grave. That's all I said, that prayer. Because after six years of being on the street, I was coming to the end of my homelessness, even if it meant suicide.

Not long after, I found myself on Spadina Avenue one morning, near Dundas in Chinatown. We used to go there to buy Chinese cooking wine, but it was still early. As I was walking along, my eyes came to rest on a sign saying Spadina Avenue. *Spadina?* What does that mean? My hungover vision began to focus, and suddenly a brilliant beam of light shone down to my very dark soul. The sign told me that her original name was Eshpadinaa. But I was taught to be ashamed of being Anishinaabe; to be ashamed of speaking the original language on this great part of Turtle Island called Canada.

Standing there on the avenue with ghosts, I cried out to Creator, "*Give me life or death, no matter how! Do whatever it takes! I don't give a shit.*" I needed change. I needed direction. And then Eshpadinaa began teaching me.

I immediately knew that my test involved a series of steps.

I went back to this park where my friends were. They were all gathered, waiting for post time—that's when the wine shops open up—ten o'clock—that's what we call post time. But I had a feeling I'd never see these faces again. I looked at each and every one of them. And then I walked away.

I walked all the way to Anishinaabe Health Toronto—there was a social worker there named Alex Jacobs. I had met Alex on his street patrol, and that is when things began to change when it came to trust. Alex would hand out coffee and hot soup, but he never preached or tried to get me off the street. He was just looking after us—handing out food and then he was gone. So trust had built up over the winter, to believe this guy that appeared every night; that he would be there every spring, summer. He became a fixture, and that paved the way to eventually say, "Okay, let's go see him."

I walked into Alex's office and said, "I have to sober up, man. I've had it." Alex took me to St. Jude's detox and from there to the Native Men's Residence. Before that, I'd not wanted much to do with Native men in Toronto because I was ashamed of being a Native man. But then here I was, living with these Native men—who I had always thought were a bunch of losers. From there, I began to feel this Nativeness; it started to come back to me.

I went from the Native Men's Residence into Pedahbun Lodge, a rehab centre for Native people. In my residual memory, I knew pedahbun as *biidaaban*, dawn comes. See how the language was coming towards me? Biidaaban means dawn or the spreading. You can see the line of light in the horizon, the lights spreading around. It's coming this way, that's what biidaaban means.

How sobering that is, the power behind these words.

Anishinaabeg is my nation. As my Anishinaabe soul began to shine, my head was spinning with very graphic word bundles. Zaagajiwe (walking over the hill). Ogidaaki (on top of a hill). Bikwadinaa (a small hill). The very language that I was taught to be ashamed of had become my salvation, my deliverance from the cold-blooded city streets.

So, that word Eshpadinaa has been very significant on my journey. Because you worship the Creator on a high hill, on a high place. And I've been climbing the hill ever since.

Shibendamowin, Perseverance

Shibe (stretch out towards); bendamo (mental concentration); win (state).

My son learned to crawl backwards, but he got stuck under things. One day, he was reaching out for something—and he learned to crawl forwards, and walk, and run!

Pedahbun Lodge

I was in rehab for eight months at Pedahbun Lodge before things finally broke. I had built such a big thick wall aound myself over the years that there wasn't even a crack there. My treatment wasn't going well—until that one beautiful morning.

I was sitting with a bunch of the Pedahbun residents and I remember suddenly getting up to leave the group. I stood up and said, "You're better off without me. I'm leaving, guys." I took off upstairs and started looking for garbage bags to put my stuff in. My plan was to go back to Bathurst and Queen, and my feeling was *Screw it all!* But nobody had a garbage bag! I knew the centre had lots of black garbage bags, and I was thinking *at least they could spare one or two.* But nobody gave me one; they just said, "I'm sorry."

I was really angry at that point and went and sat in the visiting room where they were going to start the morning circle. As I was sitting there, one of the counsellors, Terry Swan, walked in with another friend who was a resident. My friend was doing terribly, just like me. They sat down on each side of me, and then Terry said, "I notice that every time someone graduates from Pedahbun Lodge you are very, very angry."

All of a sudden I felt the rage coming, from the bottom of my stomach, entering my chest and moving up into my throat like a huge flood. It bubbled up, right through my head and my eyes, blinding me. It was like a bad TV screen—like static. I never knew rage had a noise—like a terrible TV reception, and then there was a loud crackling. But as it moved through my neck I got flooded out, my eyes let go and I let out this really soulful cry. Once I started I couldn't stop; that medicine wheel they were telling me about was working in my soul.

You know, a tough guy like me, a street-smart guy, you don't cry. I was taught that. I'm a tough guy. I've done time. But that teaching just flew right out the window and I wasn't ashamed to cry in front of those women. Then they were crying and I started to bubble up again. It was craziness; I thought I was going crazy, because this bubble was now a different kind of crying. Maybe it was joy, I don't remember. There was just water everywhere. I was crying laughing at the same time, saying, "I'm crazy, I'm crazy!!"

But Terry said, "You know, when people leave you are angry." And my friend on the other side said something else: "Rene, you were the one that was telling me the other day we must face up to our issues. Be brave, be courageous, face them, you know, meet our problems head on. You're the guy that told me that. And now you're running away."

There were more people arriving in the group—it was time for morning circle and all the residents and counsellors were there. At one point everybody started touching me on my back. I guess I was kneeling and then I could hear women sobbing. I wondered to myself, *What are they crying about?* When I felt this gentle touch on my back, I didn't swing around to hit, as I might have done in the past. But I must have been swearing when I was under the flood because at one point someone threw a punching bag on the floor. They told me later that they were afraid I might break my hands and wrists because I was hitting that punching bag so hard, letting the rage out.

After I was finished they all came and helped me up, and when they did I felt so light. It was like this weight on my back shattered and lifted away from me, and I kept rising. I felt the ground for the first time; the cement floor felt like soft, springy moss. That's when I understood the expression of emotion and the healing began immediately. I got up and just said, "Wow." As the women hugged me I said, "Okay, I'm staying."

I realized that I had this abandonment issue, starting from when my mother went to the sanitarium for tuberculosis when I was a kid. She had promised she'd come back, but that's when my family was split up. My brother went to one grandmother, and I went to the other. I finally understood that was where the abandonment started, and as Terry pointed out, every time a client graduated from Pedahbun Lodge, they were abandoning me again. The people at Pedahbun were my family, and I felt, *This can't happen again, no.* So I was always trying to hold them back, trying to keep everybody.

After that crying, the medicine started to work. I was about forty at that time, and I had never cried. But since then I'm not afraid to cry.

Eshkonedj, Survivor

Eshko (remain); onedj (from death).

I am Eshkonedj of the Indian residential school and its "To kill the Indian in the child" policies.

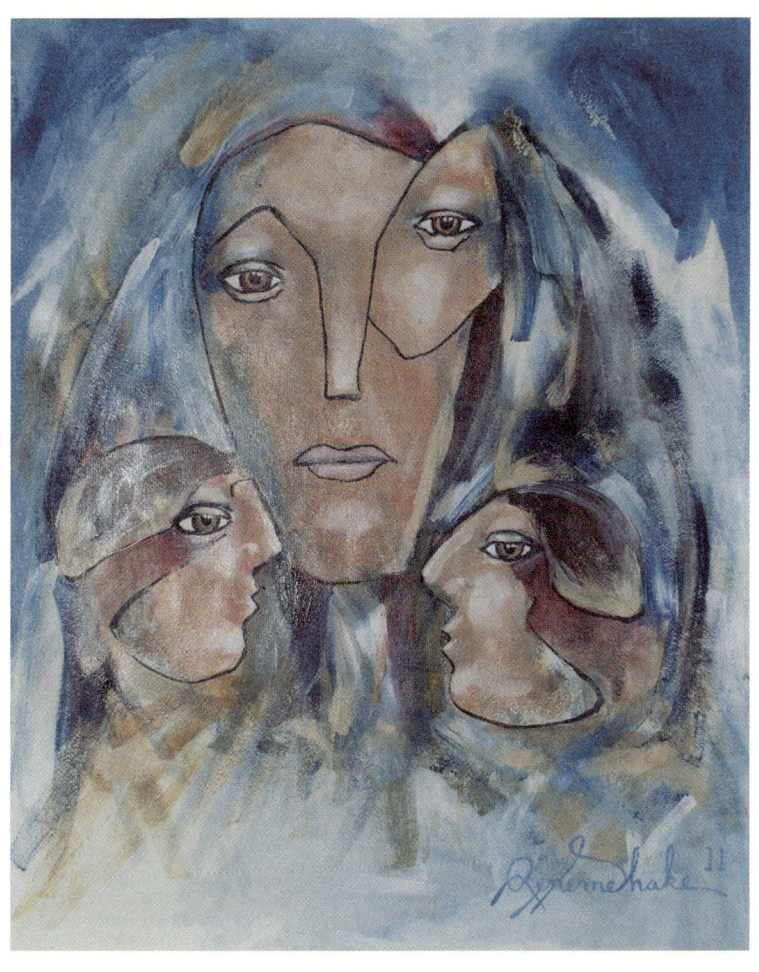

Sidogawishkode, To Balance a Canoe, 2011, acrylic on paper, 33 x 43.2 cm.

Buffalo Child

A bull of a wave
charged onshore and spun,
breaking up water to lave
and fall before my little son.
He shook his baby fists
in the air, shouting,
"Freedom, freedom!"
I saw mists of Lake Superior rerouting.
I saw the buffalo surge retreat,
putting down the mist
like a carpet at his feet,
the command of a baby's fist.

Gige, Heal

Gi (with); ige (wound healing).

In and through community is Gige, our healing. When your sons and daughters are going through some darkness, only your love will bring them to the other side.

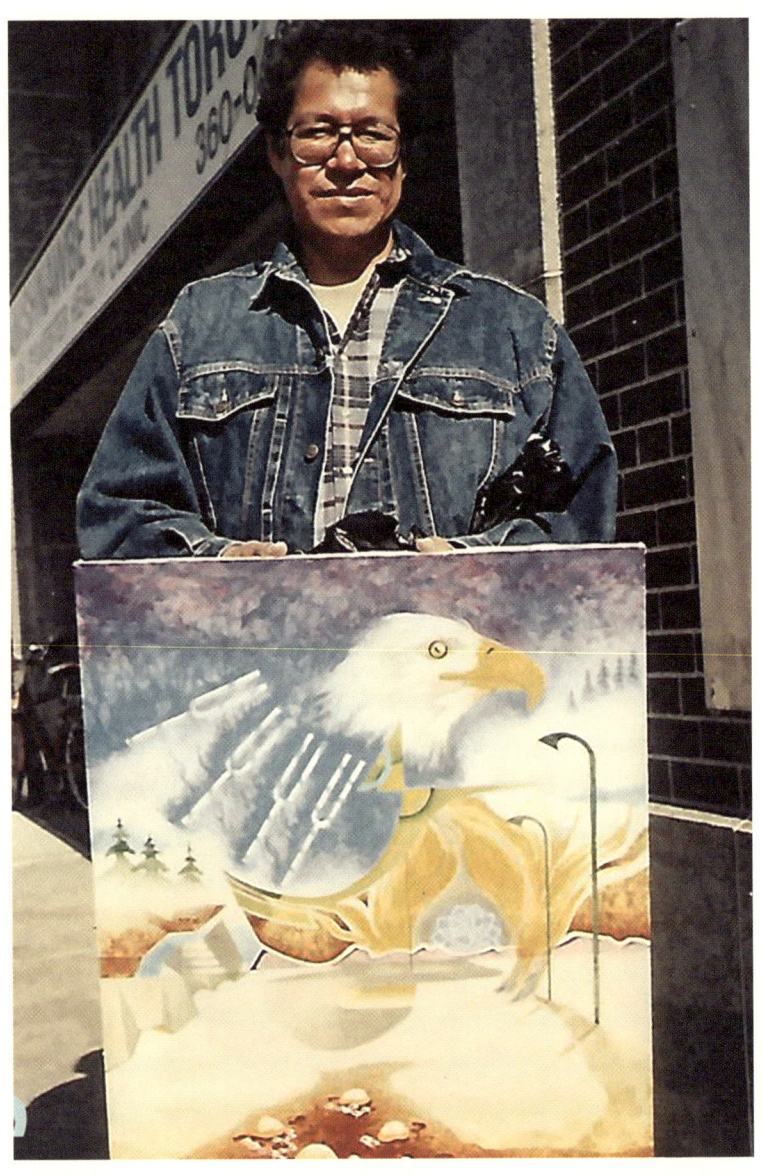

Rene outside of Anishinaabe Health Toronto, c. 1991, with the painting that travelled to Australia. Photo by Joan Bruder.

Brain Check

At Pedahbun Lodge my counsellor told me that every time that I passed out I killed my brain cells. I became obsessed, wondering, *how many times had I passed out?* I had to find out if I had any brain cells left.

I first volunteered at a non-profit organization to prove that I still had my mind. My job was to sort, package, and mail reading resource materials, and I did this for a whole year. I kept records too. No one complained; the mail must have reached its destination.

There was then another test. Painting. Had I forgotten my palette? Could I paint again? It would require colour theory, mathematics, geometry, space, foreshadowing, perspective, design, and the right mix of lightness, saturation, and hue to bring my artwork to life. Then this lady came along and commissioned me to create a painting for her brother. She was going to Australia to visit him. When she saw the painting she stopped, entranced, and her face lit up—and when she came back to Canada she told me a story about how the Indigenous Australians came to her brother's house to see the painting. They had never done that before, and I had never been so pleased in all my life. Her story confirmed that I could still paint.

I recovered more and began a new life. I volunteered again, this time for United Way Toronto to launch their annual campaign. Instead, I found myself being interviewed for a documentary. They even provided me with a chauffeur of my own, an RV trailer, a makeup artist, and snack and beverage service. As I was sitting in my RV, some people came along, pointed at me and gestured martial arts. They thought that I was making a martial arts movie. Eeee-yah!

Next thing I knew, I was a poster boy for the United Way Toronto campaign. Posters of my face were plastered all over the subway stations. I was tempted to walk over there and pose next to the poster and say, "Spare change?" I could picture pedestrians doing a double take: *Isn't that him?*

But it was all in check. I had asked Creator to do whatever it takes. Miigwetch apitchi, Gichi-Manidoo.

Shawendjigewin, Grace

Shawan (south); endjige (focus one's attention on); ewin (state).

I just love the way the Old Ones describe grace. Like you're bringing the whole south wind on someone's hard times when you show mercy! Gichi Manidoo (Grand Mystery), grace is like that. I've known it for twenty-seven sober years now.

Baapinakamigad, Festivities

Baapi (laugh); nakami (relate to earth); gad (at present).
Laughter is an instant medicine. It is a festival of festivities!

Naagidisowin

When I sobered up, I had this one determination—to be financially independent. I didn't know how I was going to do it; I couldn't see beyond Bathurst and Queen and I had no sense of control over my life because I had been brought up in the system. Indian Affairs was always in control; the educational system was in control. But there was a threshold at one point when I said, "This is not working." I was in a place where alcohol had taken so much control that I was homeless, in jail, drifting. I saw myself as a loser, and there was this great dark void of nothingness. Emptiness. Like nobody is listening; I don't have a voice—*who gives a shit?* That's exactly how I felt.

The day I decided to sober up I knew I had to find meaning in my life, but it didn't happen right away. I struggled for eight months in rehab at Pedahbun Lodge while the work of my vision quest began.

The first thing I had to do was give something up, and that was drugs and alcohol. Then even the friends I had hung out with—I had to give them up too. I learned that my vision quest required developing a new sense of belonging, and that's work—it's hard to leave all these comfortable things behind when you go on a vision quest. But for the first time in my life I began to really think about what it means to be Anishinaabe. Maybe it had started with that talk the Elder (Stan Fontaine) gave me in Winnipeg, about the medicine wheel. The wheel came back to me in Pedahbun Lodge, and I'll introduce how it was done.

SELF-EMPLOYMENT = ANOKIWIN

LIFE-CHANGING
MOVEMENT:
andji-bimadisiwin
OR *mamaasikaa*

PASSION
naagidisowin

VISION
moshitowin

PERSEVERANCE
shibendamowin

The ancestors call it naagidisowin. That's vision quest. When somebody asks me naagidisowin, it's *how do you see yourself?* Today I have naagidso. It's how you see yourself, let's say seven generations from now, or tomorrow, the next week, the next month, the next year, the next ten years. How do you see yourself?

I now see myself as an artist. I see myself as a poet. I see myself as a writer. I see myself making use of all the talents that God gave me, to enlighten people, to heal people, to elevate culture.

The next step is to persevere, and the ancestors called it shibenda-mowin. Shibendam is to apply your mind. It is the strength of your mind and all your abilities. The strength of your talents. That's what I see, the strength of my talents, and the ability to strengthen them to practise. Photoshop, photography, research, sketching. My eagles, my bears, my characters. Developing characters, giving them life. That is shibendam—strengthening my talents and abilities.

Then there's the third direction: passion. Be passionate about this. The ancestors gave me this word moshitowin. That's this passion within me. Mosh is to feel; feel this taking shape and to get this movement.

Finally, I like to use this word andji-bimaadiziwin. It means life-changing movement. That's the fourth direction: andji-bimaadiz-iwin. Andji means change. Bimaadiziwin means life. It's a life-changing movement that's been happening in my life.

For me, that wheel changed my life, and has kept me going for the last twenty-seven years of being self-employed and beholden to no one.

My biggest regret is that the rez doesn't commonly send off the young people into the forest to seek a vision. But I think you could still do it later. I did, and it was like what my ancestors did to seek a vision for life. That vision is education, employment, or labour—your dodem. I didn't go out to the bush and fast; I just did it in the city, with Pedahbun Lodge when they said, "Don't worry about anything (food, a room, etc.); just concentrate on yourself." So I entered their teaching lodge. I had counsellors; it was a form of going into the forest because I didn't have to worry about where my next meal was coming from or how I was going to change my clothes. I just concentrated on my vision, my healing.

In this vision quest you are given a guiding spirit, and the spirit that was really strong for me was the lamb of God. I'm not ashamed of that because I was given Yeshua, and the community has to respect that. In the old days, the Elders would be sitting around, and a young woman or man would come back and say, "This is my guiding spirit; this is my vision," and they were respected for that. And it worked for me.

That was missing when I went to high school. Nobody there talked about spiritual things and so my education meant nothing to me. I never produced works of art on the rez because I couldn't see; all I saw before me was a bottle of wine. I had opportunities to work with people in the commercial world, but I couldn't see anything other than money, and money sometimes just clouds the vision. Then there's alcohol, which is the worst thing that can cloud your vision. Forget it. And if you do drugs and try to seek a vision you will never find it.

Now we have all these suicides, even young kids, twelve, thirteen. Maybe we could be encouraging more to go to the forest to seek a vision. We could tell them, "a spirit guide will be given to you; maybe a wolf or a bear—that's the mystery—and the bush is right there—you can still do it." That's what I think is missing when I hear about suicides. I've been there; I've been to suicide, but I saw myself through. It was finding that Naagidso, which means how you see yourself—your identity.

I'm still not done because it's my lifetime work. It's perseverance and passion, even at seventy; that's the fuel that will move you forward into life-changing environments.

Gagonsonge, Inspire

Gagans (steady); songe (strengthening).
Inspiration begins with the steady strengthening of community.

The Pipigwan Flute

There is a story about how the flute was given to us. It happened one time when this young guy fell in love with a beautiful girl, but he had nothing. Other guys had horses and canoes—they were great hunters, they were wrestlers, dancers, drummers, singers—all this stuff. But he had nothing, and the girl wanted nothing to do with him. So he wandered off into the forest, heartbroken.

He sat down beside this big tree and started crying, and above him one of the branches started blowing. The winds heard him and felt sorry for him, asking, "What are we going to do?" As they said this they blew harder against the branch, so hard that the bark came off.

Nearby, there was a bird we call pipigwis—the woodpecker, the one that flickers, and when he flies you see this flash of yellow and green. So pipigwis was flying through the pine trees making a sound, like the one he does really loud in the morning. He landed on the branch beside the young guy who was crying and started pecking holes in the branch. As he did this, the winds blew harder, and the branch fell off, landing right beside the young guy, on top of a bush.

The guy thought, *What is this?* He was really curious about the sounds he had heard coming from it. He picked it up, thinking, *I'm going to go back to the village one more time just to get one more glimpse of the girl.*

As he started walking, he heard this big noise coming from an elk. He looked and saw that there was a herd of females all gathered around this elk and became transfixed by this vision before him. When the elk walked away, all the female elk followed him. So, okay, the young man thought to himself, *that has something to do with courting female elks.* He then thought, *maybe I can try making music by the river, where the girl usually comes to get her water in the morning.*

He went back to the village and began playing the branch instrument that pipigwis had made. And when the girl heard it, she came by and said, "Oh what a beautiful sound! It doesn't sound like a bird; it doesn't sound like anything I've ever heard before!" She peeked through the bushes and saw the young man sitting there, playing the flute.

"You love it?" he asked. "I'm just practising." And then he played some more. "Well, if you love my music," he said, "will you marry me? If you don't like it, that's the last you will ever see of me. I will just go far, far away, where nobody will ever hear this again."

But the girl said "I'll marry you"—and that's how the instrument came to be a courting instrument for guys. That young guy went on and learned how to play really happy songs, and then he taught everybody else in this village how to play.

I think when you are brought up in the forest, it's not only the people, like the aunts and uncles, that raise you up. It's the birds, the elks, the trees, and the wood, the wind; this is the music, the medicine.

Pipigwan is the name given to the traditional flute. I never heard it played in the '40s, '50s, '60s—nobody played it anymore—not my uncles or my grandfather; I just heard stories about it. You know what happened to these flutes when the missionaries came to our relatives? The music died, and the people started singing hymns instead.

But pipigwan still speaks, and it has its own language called pipigwe. Pipigwe is to speak the language of love to the women. It could be to your wife, or to your aunts, to your sisters. The man was responsible for playing music.

I have my own story about how pipigwan came back.

Joan and I had just gotten married and we were living by the river. One day, as I was looking through our big bay window, I saw the fog gradually opening, like curtains drawing. Then I saw a bird soar across the opening and evaporate into the mist. I didn't know what it was. It looked like a hawk, but I didn't pay much attention to it.

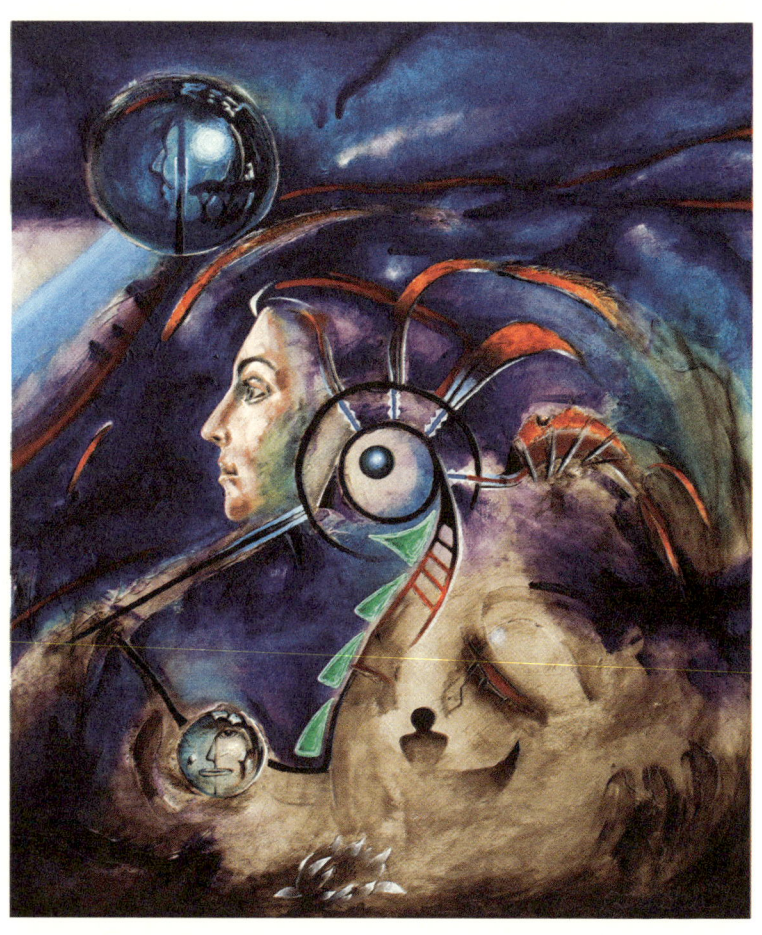

Pipigwewin, Flute, 2011, acrylic on canvas, 76.2 x 91.4 cm.

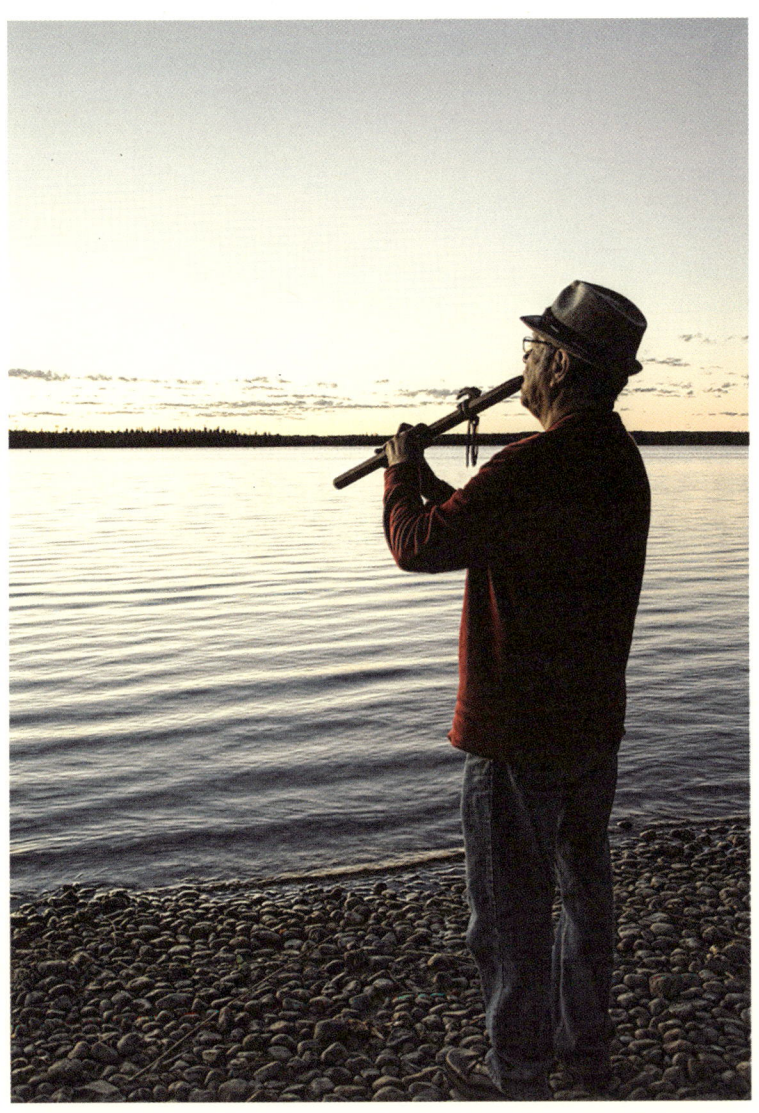
Rene and his Pipigwan, Anderson Lake, Ontario, 2015. Photo by Joan Bruder

I had forgotten that vision until years later, when I was at an Indigenous heritage festival at a local high school. The word "heritage" had gotten my attention and drawn me there. Heritage would be anikeshkagewin in my language. Anikeshkage (to follow after another), win (state). What was I following? Anikeshkage to what?

After I struck up my booth (selling my children's books), I took some time to browse the other vendors. I saw this guy with a flute on his table on a little stand, and I walked over because it was calling me. With a nod of my head, my eyes fixated on it. It pulsated with a shine and spoke to me. I had never wanted any instrument in my life so bad. So I asked him if he accepted debit cards. No. Visa? No.

He wanted cash. Being Anishinaabe, I had no cash. I raced across the gymnasium to my booth and began selling my books in earnest. As soon as I made enough money, I walked back across to him. I picked up the flute, gave him his cash and walked away, feeling, *I really got something*. I was so happy I was dancing back to my booth, but then I stopped and said to him, "By the way, what's the name of the flute?" He said, "Red-tailed hawk."

Then I had this epiphany and that vision came back. I realized the bird that had soared across the opening in the mist was the red-tailed hawk. I stood frozen on the floor. I held a red-tailed hawk pipigwan flute in my hands.

Now, I didn't know how to play the flute. Growing up on the rez, no one played pipigwan. When the missionaries came, the pipigwan flute-playing tradition was abandoned. And who were the missionaries? Jesuits. And there I was in Guelph, living near the Jesuit centre that has acres of fields and meadows with a creek going by. I drove over there, parked and got this flute out. There is a graveyard of Jesuits there too, and now here I was, with the people who caused the music to die. It healed me and made me laugh from my heart.

I took my pipigwan out and went into the cornfields and began practising scales. The birds came chirping and fluttering around me and I began to mimic their songs. The crickets and insects kept time. Before long, I found myself jamming with the birds and crickets. I thought, *I may not have known traditional Anishinaabe flute songs, but it's no big deal. The birds and the crickets are teaching me! Nita pipigwew. I speak pipigwan language now. The magic begins when the pipigwan melodies induce in my head visualizations moving in colour and shapes and vice versa!*

Then some women walked by and called out, "That's pretty good!"

"No, no, I'm just practising!" I decided I needed to get away from women and everybody else, so I drove to another parking lot out by what used to be a railroad track. I thought I was deep in the bush, riding the free roads and I could just play the flute. But then I saw a big German shepherd looking at me. And guess what? A woman crawls out of the bush, and says, "That was pretty great!"

So I figured I can't play in private anymore. And now that I have this flute, what am I going to do with it?

Make the turtle dance.

Caress Me Recipe

While my stock
and peas are slicking,
you stir by the clock
to hamper sticking.
You nip my eggplant
into bite-sized chunks
madly scant
for salted dunks.
Drain my eggplant,
rinse and pat dry
almonds, onions, and chant,
"A chili, chili fly."
Brown in your pan
to thicken my peas
with the heated bran
and steamy wheeze.
Spices, peaches, fried
ingredients stew
too hot to ride
and subdue.
Yet, you serve with delight
till your rice be a simmered gel,
then leave me overnight
knowing,
I keep and reheat well.

Lily

None compares
with the way you roll
and sing your airs
in the wilds of my soul.
Exulted
in our new school
of your quiet
lily bloom in the pool.

Renewal: Reconnection

I've done Time and when I got out, I was still doing Time; colonialism time, materialism time. Colonialism was telling me, "You are inferior. Let us take control of your life and it will be better," and materialism was telling me, "You are inferior. Buy these products and they will make you a better man." I was primed! Nothing got better. Nothing changed.

Even depression and anxiety kept me locked up. I was always renting rooms that looked like my jail cell. You know? Four walls, a closet, a window, a chair and table, and a bed. (That's if I had enough money.) My biggest fear was going without a drink in my hand.

One time, a sergeant said to me, "You don't belong here," while I was in jail. Of all the times that I been incarcerated, no one ever told me that I didn't belong there. When it came from a white sergeant, I was incredulous. And another time, a judge said to me, "I've never heard him say that!" The Crown prosecutor beside us had said, "I'm impressed!" I was making efforts to stay clean and sober at a rehab at the time. From unexpected places, I was getting the message that I was finally doing something right. Something different. I was reconnecting with something with a future. Something meaningful.

I began to have a vision! After eight months of rehab, I was going to create and design sets for the theatre. I needed a resumé. I needed theatre experience. But computers were the rage at that time and so I took a course in a microcomputer clerk training program. Now, I didn't even know how to type! They said, "You're just the guy that we're looking for." I completed the course in June 1993, never missing a day. It was the first, most meaningful work of my life. Satisfying, since I was getting paid to learn, too. I learned to keyboard by borrowing a typewriter and practising after school for three or four hours in the evenings till I got it right. I could type at least twenty-five words a minute! For the first time in my life, I felt a sense of status—I'm my own boss. No one was telling me what to do. I even became a tutor in microcomputer clerk training. I was reconnected to anokiiwin, which means work. It was my choice and I was making a difference. I chose to keep working hard because I saw myself making and exploring creative arts using computers as far as five or more years ahead. I was primed! I was reconnected!

Next thing you know, I was married. I was determined to be financially independent. I built my own multimedia home studio. My gracious wife sold her dining room furniture to make room in the dining room for my PC and Mac computers and cables all over the place. I taught myself Photoshop, Illustrator, InDesign, Final Cut Pro, and Logic Pro X. I could edit images and music in my new-found world. I created using integrated art forms with emphasis on my Anishinaabe heritage without creative compromise. I'd come to know the value of anokiiwin, or better still, anokiitaazo (self-employment). No one could fire me; I had a future!

I felt less anxious and less depressed as I grew my business, even as I struggled making art. One painting wasn't working out and I kept throwing it to the corner. After two years of revisions, I decided to paint over it. As I scrubbed away the layers of paint, an image of a woman emerged. Hers was a story of patience. I titled the painting *Patience*. It inspired a line of greeting cards that I sold at farmers' markets, festivals, trade shows, and arts and crafts shows. One of the benefits of participating in a show was instant community; instant camaraderie with fellow vendors. We watched over each other's stuff when someone took a break. We were less anxious. I met and networked with teachers.

Soon I was presenting and workshopping Ojibwe arts, language, and culture in the classrooms. I was in my element; I belonged.

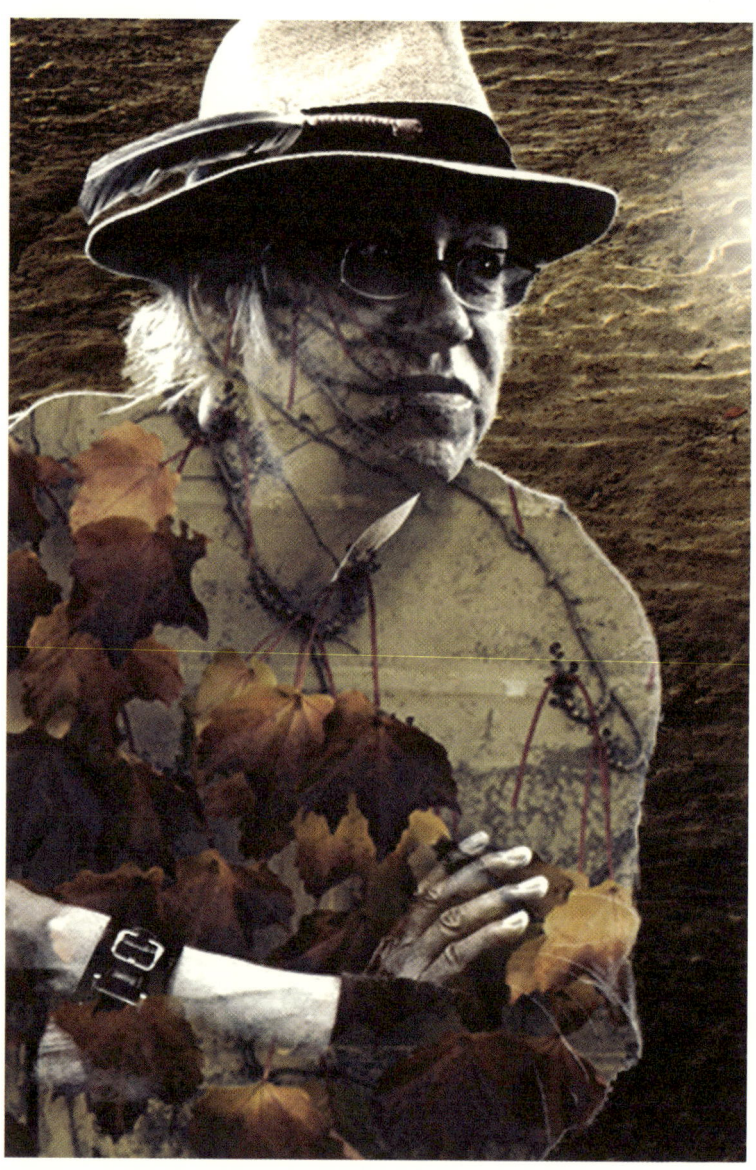

Ininatigobag, Leafy, 2018, digital multimedia.

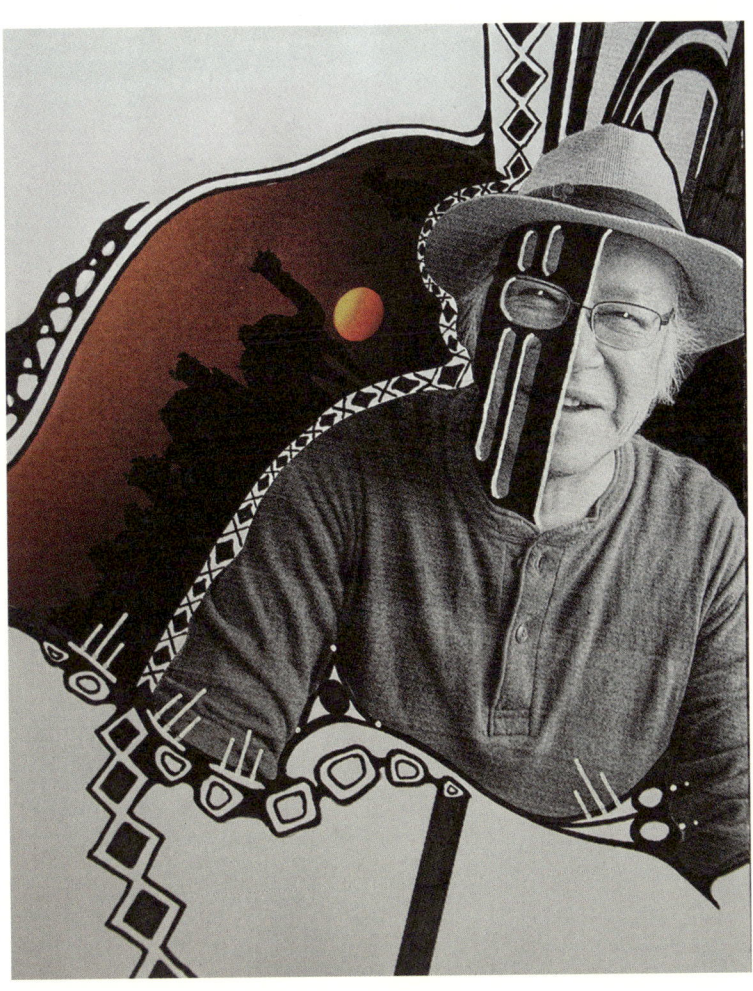

Self-portrait, 2016, collage on paper.

My wife even quit her day job and partnered with me. Together we've amassed a body of work that has already taken us to Barcelona, Catalonia, and Dublin, Ireland. Personally, I had blossomed by receiving recognition from my wife, family, friends in academia, and the arts community. I couldn't do it alone! My social connections made it possible to compete with the world. Hey man! I was primed.

The vision quest is an intricate thing to understand. It demanded fasting from me; I fasted from alcohol and tobacco. I'm still fasting. It's been twenty-seven years now. My quest led me to participate in a Screenwriting Workshop for Aboriginal Storytellers at the Banff Centre for the Arts in September 2000. It was there that I had a mystical experience and understood the power of nature. After my script was read and I heard the words—"I see a writer in here," I took a walk up the hill. I saw a ten-year-old boy sitting still, downcast, and full of shame at his desk. He had been molested. He had stopped writing. He had stopped living. I approached him, patted his shoulders, took his hand, and said to him, "Come with me! We are going to write stories!" As we stood on the slope of our hill, the panorama of our freedom opened up before us, and we wrote our first poem. At that moment, I learned what our ancestors meant by gashki'ewisiwin: to have control over our stories! Our language is embedded in the land. Gashki'ewisiwin inspired me and my inner child to live as survivors, not victims. The ten-year-old boy taught me to listen or bizindan to my pain, follow it back, and to heal from there. The root word in bizindan is bizaan: quiet, still. It's in peace that you hear and understand things.

The following is an allegorical story about bizindan and kotagitowin, pain.

Ginebigoons, the tiny snake, curled himself under the shade of a rock. *If I get any hotter I'm going to die*, he thought. He couldn't move until everything cooled down. He was in the middle of the burned-out forest. Ashes flew by him. As soon as the temperature dropped, he crawled out.

Too much of anything is bad for me, he thought, *and so is too little of anything*. The wildfires had destroyed his homeland. No hope of regeneration. Ginebigoons longed to be like the eagle. Big and strong and free. The heat that was once friendly was oppressive. He wandered from shady patch to shady patch to survive.

Why weren't there any ginebigoog, snakes, on the land? Ginebigoons thought. *No turtles, no birds, no foxes, no one!* He felt lonely. He could be the last one, the last surviving member of his kind. The waters tasted foul. The eagle vanished from the sky.

As long as I remain tiny! A miniature snake—I will survive in this burned out forest, Ginebigoons said to himself. *I will call my new home, The Burn!*

"Debwe na?" he heard a voice say. He shook his head and blinked his eyes. *Such a sweet voice,* he thought, *but where did it come from?*

"I dare someone question my truth!" he said, "Who's there?"

"Debwe na?" the voice said again.

"The Burn has rendered us invisible," said Ginebigoons. "Everywhere The Burn migrates, it plunders."

"Debwe na?"

"Indebwe sha!" he shouted. "The Burn just takes, and takes, and takes without your permission. And I'm so mad that I want to do the same!"

"Debwe!" said the voice, "Ozhaa'washkozi, indizhinikaaz, but you can call me The Green."

"Ginebigoons, niin," he replied nervously.

"Well, Ginebigoons, since most of your kind are dead, who is left to guide you but your pain, your kotagitowin."

Ginebigoons surveyed The Burn and saw the light, the opportunity, and his anger chilled. "Should I make myself big," he said, "to make myself credible?"

"Debwe, but to whom? Most of your kind are dead."

"Ah, gi debwe, Ozhaa'washkozi," Ginebigoons nodded his head.

"Yes, Ginebigoons, go and journey into your own pain and live to tell us about it. Remember, there is a word in our language for listening, and it's bizindan. The word comes from bizaan, which means be quiet, be still and peaceful enough to hear clearly."

He lifted his head and heard the land. Ginebigoons heard the call of frogs, the chirp of birds, the whisper of wind through the trees, and beyond the trees the rush of waters. The hum. Gradually, he began to sing along, dance, and give thanks. Miigwetchi'wendan became a custom, a ritual for him each day.

Ah, the Green of our Anishinaabe future ways is in our language, songs, dances, prayers, rituals, and writings, he thought.

"Gwaiakotam Ginebigoons," The Green said. "He heard it right!"

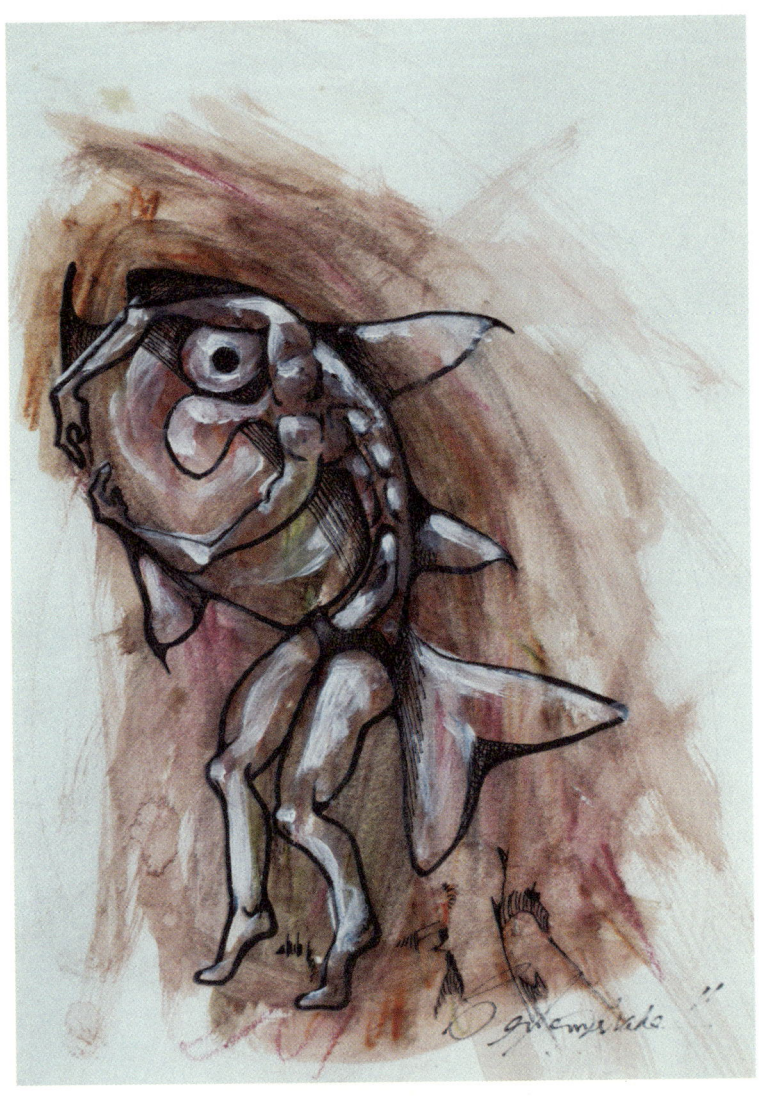

Giigoonhs, Fish, 2011, acrylic on paper, 33 x 43.2 cm.

PART SIX

Papawangani
Stories of Healing Through Art

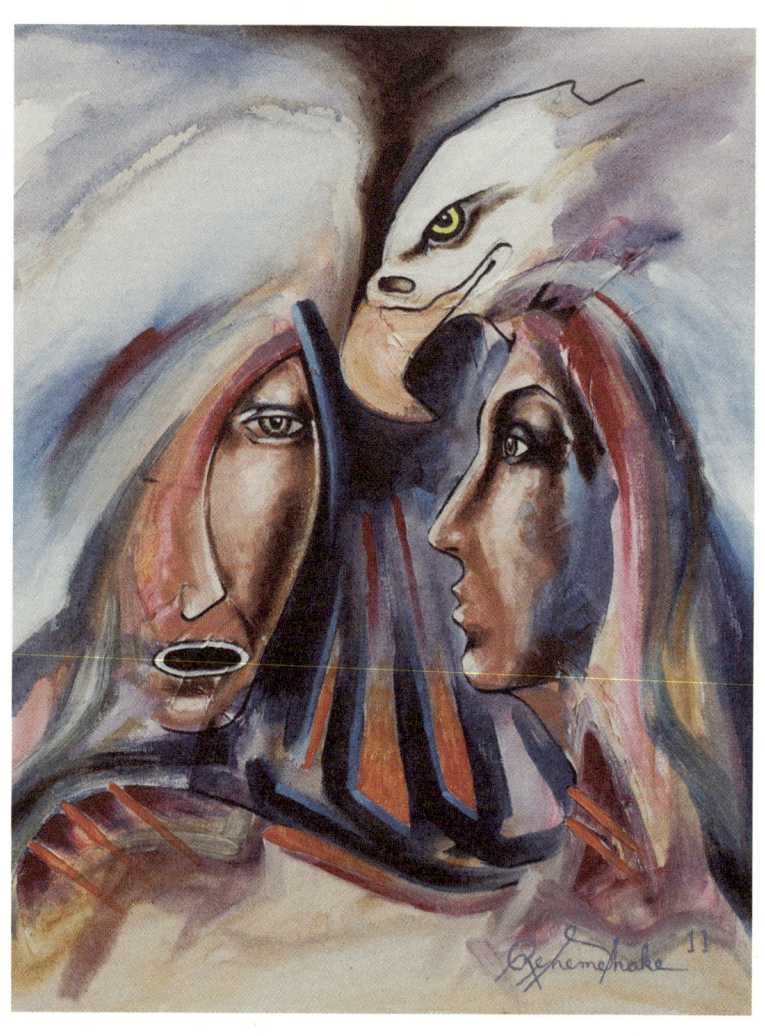

Papawangani, Quivering Wings, 2011, acrylic on canvas, 40.6 x 50.8 cm.

Papawangani

Papaw (quiver), wangani (wings).

Mishinong asha nin danamia, jibwa kikendamaan Papawangani ishinikasoian. Nogom dash, indinendis ni papawanganidan Anishinaabe Kino'amagewigaming gimodisiwin. Midash, ningwiss kawiin wika gobimiwidosiinan menishendamowin gaie wiisagendamowin. Kawiin gaie ji bishigwadenimadjan widji-Anishinaabensag.

Menishendamowin nagashka omaa!

About twenty years ago, I was sitting by my bay window as the sun was going down. I marvelled at the orange glow of everything.

It was then that I clearly heard, "Papawangani!" I turned to see if my wife was calling me. But no one was there!

I saw my green acoustic guitar leaning against the wall. Since when did my wife learn to speak Anishinaabemowin? I told her about it when she came downstairs and she said, "No, I never said anything." I started calling my guitar Papawangani.

After many prayers, I began to realize that this is my name. Papawangani. Today, I imagine myself quivering my wings to shake off the Indian residential school legacy so that my son will never bear the shame. He will never experience or inflict this shame on anyone.

The shame stops here!

All Rivers, Streams, Creeks, Sing!

Portages are called Onigam in Anishinaabemowin. That's where we got the word Nagamo—to sing. I believe that doing portages after you've been in the lakes and rivers gave you time to goji-naga-mo—practise singing the songs the rivers sang. That's culture. That's minobimadisiwin. And Zibi describes rivers as spilling out of lakes. Singing or humming is like that.

Our ancestors must have heard a lot of songs, living by the lakes and rivers. Ice can really sing when you're in a deep lake; you can hear it all night making rumbling sounds, like a drum. It talks. And if you ever go to the middle of the lake and see the northern lights you hear them hiss while the ice moves around under you, moaning. There's music. You can hear it echo down the other side of the lake, way out there.

I like the sounds of the springtime. The icicles on the shoreline make this ringing like wind chimes. There's the waves washing—rolling back and forth. That's where our language comes from. Neegamowin. The sound of the wind crying—the original blues; very mournful, like a wailing.

There were songs for everything. Even a chipmunk can have a song. You can sing to a bear, and there are spontaneous songs too. You know the mink has his song as he swims across the lake, and it ends when he disappears into the bush? If it moves there's a song for it.

So you get this symphony going, where we're all being taught to sing. It's the earth singing, it's the ice. And heaven help you if you don't sing or hum, because you become a dead pond!

Passwewe, Echo

Passwe (resound); we (voice).

Passwewe has a reverb soul when I improvise my music on my traditional pipigwan flute. The pipigwan flute has a language of its own, and it's called pipigwewin.

Aabadjichiganan,
Tool

Aabad (used over and over again); jichigan (means or tool); nan (plural).

I never dreamt that my paint brushes—aabadjichiganan—would put dinner on my table. Since I recovered from addictions, brokenness, and homelessness, indaabadjichiganan in my hands has meant self-confidence in my work as a visual artist and writer.

Boxes, Circles, and Arcs

My work as an artist goes back to the grandmothers, who used to sit around and tell stories. Us kids would listen and then we would go out and play in the dirt, making drawings inspired by what we had heard. Sometimes the girls would build little communities out of mud and invite us in to play—they were always in charge! They made pretend tea and so I drank a lot of tea. Then the rain would come and wash away all of our art and we would start over again on a new canvas.

That was woodlands art. We were all doing it, sometimes drawing on the sands, or sometimes with crayons. We didn't talk about it as art or talent; it was just part of expressing yourself, expressing the story, a certain line here or there. My grandmother always enjoyed it, telling me, "that's beautiful." I got that freedom in the bush, to draw and express whatever I wanted.

Then came the oppression of the church. They had long ago burned our instruments, taking that form of self-expression, but we never lost it all. There were things like my grandfather's songs. When we were paddling, he'd see a mink swim beside us, and he'd sing a song for it, a mink song. I didn't hear that kind of singing in church. There it became the kind of song with "Amazing Grace" in Ojibwe. The songs changed. The bush songs, they were more lively.

When I got to Long Lac Indian Day School, the nuns saw that I was a storyteller, and all the kids in my class recognized me as the artist; the one that draws best. The teacher would say, "good drawer," and put all these little golden stars on my drawings. When I was good in class she would wipe the chalkboard clean so I could make big drawings. But something had changed. I was required to draw differently; more Catholic stuff. I became a Catholic artist.

I did perfect 3D hearts and crosses, Christmas trees, houses—I could do all that. I was allowed to draw the church, but I couldn't put an eagle behind it, or on Santa's shoulder, or what I saw. At best I could sneak in an owl on a Christmas tree. It wasn't long before my art became suppressed because I was never allowed to express what was Native.

That's the form of government and rules that were imposed on us. One is the natural one, and we had to adapt to the other. Drop all the most expressive lines and verses, the instantaneous happy dance kind of things. It had to be all these boxy things. And it was all these boxy things that derailed generations of us. The day schools and Indian residential schools told us, "Your culture is inferior." They loved saying that to us. Then they told us, "This is art. The way you do art is inferior."

It's so hard to get rid of that. And then, how can we pass down what we consider inferior? We end up trying to pass down Picassos and Cézannes and Andy Warhol kind of painting. Our people—and Canada—really lost out on arts and culture, because we had a lot of talent that was killed in those schools. Think of what would have happened if we weren't abused, or if we had gone to schools where they encouraged us to speak our languages and paint and write stories; where they had really looked after our young minds and talents. Canada could have done a lot but it didn't.

I kept going on with my art, though, enrolling to study at Sheridan College once I finished high school. Because of the suppression of my vision as an Anishinaabe artist, I arrived at Sheridan painting everything classical—you know, still lifes; things like an orange. My art teachers had taught me to paint every pore of that orange, and so it had become boring to do my art because everything was photographic. I thought that was art: just painting candles, Christmas trees, light bulbs, and crosses. In residential school, and later on at my high school in Thunder Bay, that's what got you an A+; that's what got me into Sheridan.

At Sheridan, though, everything changed, and it happened when I first saw Salvador Dali. Dali just blew it all away—it's like he came there and messed up my art. Took an orange right out of the peeling or that peeling grew up into a candle or found the half circles in an orange. Cut it up, squeeze it, let water come out of it. All that freed me, and I started painting surrealism. It was symbolic and a better way of merging cultures and ideas, because Ojibwe art is mostly symbolic. Circles, quarters, arcs and all; they start to tell a story. It all comes around.

In 2014, almost fifty years after my arrival at Sheridan, it came around again when I had a chance to go to Dali's homeland. It was a journey of reconciling. Kim Anderson and I were invited to talk at a conference about borders, memory, and exile. I had never wanted to cross that ocean, but I decided it was time to go back to the source of suppression, the continent where Columbus set sail. It was a journey of forgiveness, and, like Dali's art, it was freeing.

I remember arriving in Barcelona and seeing the language of Dali's people embedded in the architecture. You can see it in the scroll effect, the bulging, the curves: Catalan started to speak to me when I saw all these semi-circles and swirls, lines built for speaking. I was really awestruck by the doors and gates too. Some were forbidden to enter, and some were open—like when I'm sketching, there are lines I don't want to go over; there are lines where I can explore. That's how I internalized all those images; they were telling me stories.

I thought about the Catalan people coming to the rez—or to the forests and lakes and rivers and islands and pine trees and all this vast nature. They would see no buildings, just a flat line of muskeg. I wondered what kind of story a Catalan artist or writer would tell me if we went out there to fish for our supper. I think they would say, "This is what your land is telling me."

When we were in Barcelona we made a day trip to see the Salvador Dali museum. I was excited to read his original handprints, his hand, his strokes, knowing that as I looked at his paintings they would tell me a story. I wondered if Dali or other European artists ever thought about us when they were painting their originals: "There's going to

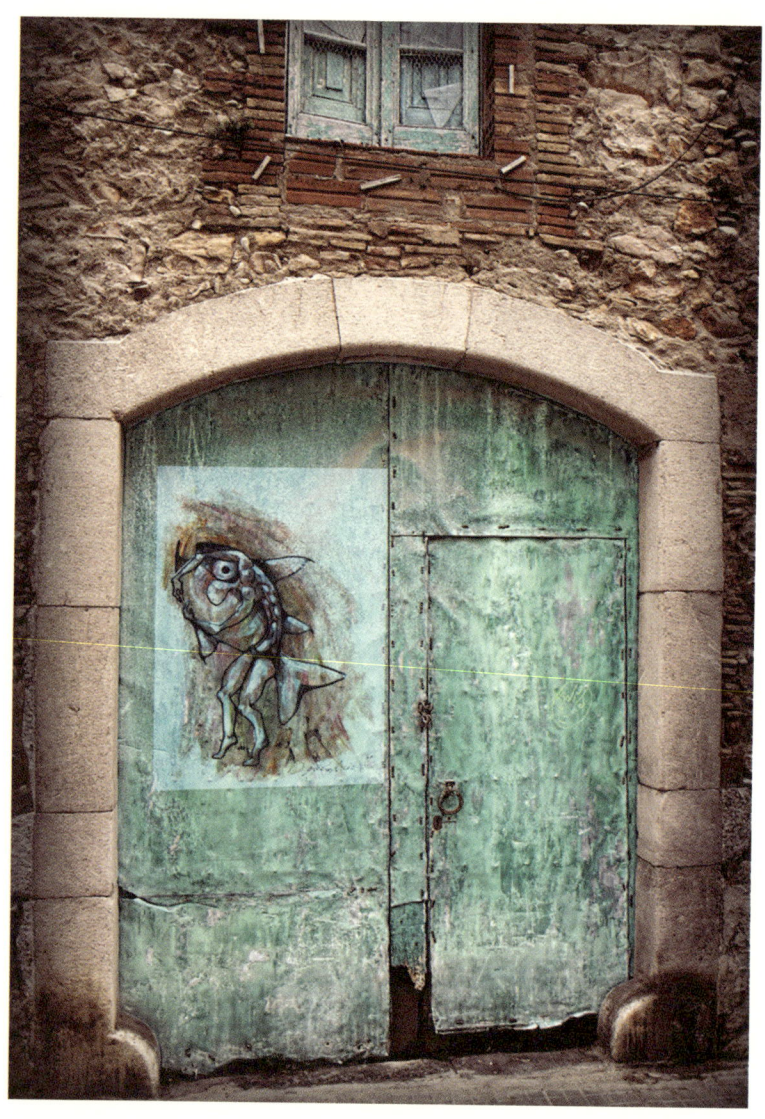

Barcelona, 2014, multimedia.

be an Anishinaabe coming over here and getting inspired." It seemed like my soul travelled ahead of me thinking of all of that, and then I felt a layer of pain and trauma peel away. That's what we're talking about here. Peelings after peelings. Survival has to do with that; trying to survive every day and wondering, *when do I pull off the last peel of the onion.*

Later in the trip we also went for a visit to Dali's home, and as I stood in his studio I felt another layer peel off. Art, language, forgiveness. That's what that trip was about.

I think all of us artists are responsible for what we put out there. Because some young person is going to come along and see your work and say, "Oh, wow," and it sets him or her free. We've got to put stuff out there, no matter how unpopular it's going to be. We have to be true to ourselves.

So that's how I see my work now. Not everybody's going to like Rene's work. I'm going to be criticized. It's like that word godjiwisiwin—which means trial. Godji means testing you, it's wrestling you, it's suffering and injustice, it's criticism, it's harsh, and it hurts like crazy. Wisi is you: it's your body taking the brunt of it; your mental, spiritual, physical life. It's emotional when all those things are attacked. And then when you iwisiwin, it's moulding you, shaping you. You become stronger, mashkawisi. You pass the exam in this university of life.

Nandomakomeshi, Monkey

Nando (hunt); mako (dig out); meshi (creature).

Nandomakome is to search for lice on someone's head. Nando-makomeshi was sometimes a performer that wore a birchbark mask (Wigwaas-wingewegan).

Waasenamawa, Enlighten

Waase (light); nam (breath); mawa (assist them).

Every now and then a waase (light carrier) walks through our communities and they assist us to breathe much better. This is enlightenment in the Anishinaabeg Nation.

Mishoomis and the Drum

There wasn't any pow-wow in Geraldton in the '70s. There was no pow-wow; nothing. And that's when Mishoomis started doing things like making this drum.

"I'm going to make a drum today." That's how it started. We went to the bush with him to cut down a tree—I think it was a birch tree. We made it into a board, boiled it, and then we wrapped the board around this big gas drum to make it round. Then there was the moose hide—we had that. Everything had to do with water; I guess he was birthing his own drum. We boiled water so he could form this drum, and of course the hide was in water, and all the rope he needed to tie the drum up or stretch it.

I helped cut the tree down and bring it back, but I never knew what he was doing. I just did whatever he told me to do. At that time, though, I was never interested in the culture. But all along he would ask, "Can you help me?" "Oh no, I'm too busy, Mishoomis . . . I have to go somewhere." Making excuses. I think sometimes he was very angry with me, but he never knew what was wrong. I never told him about the abuses at Indian residential school; he never knew. Never told him about it. Never. I think that's the main reason I didn't want to help out.

It's amazing too, when I look back at what he did. In my generation, we didn't care about practising anything cultural. At that time, we even prostituted art. That's what I call it now, I did art just to get drunk. I sold pieces just for a case of beer or a bottle of wine, and Mishoomis saw me do that. "Aniin . . . you went to an art school and you come back here and you're partying all the time," he'd say.

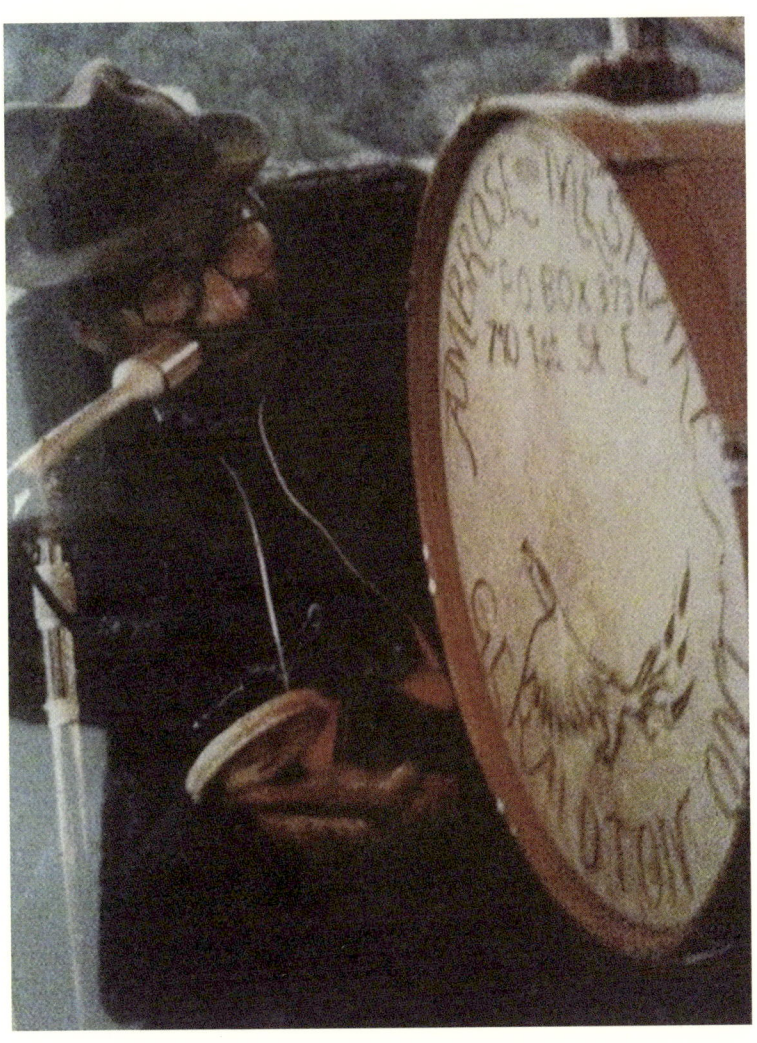

Mishoomis Ambrose and his drum, c. mid-1970s. Credit: Meshake family archives.

After Mishoomis made his drum, he bought an amplifier and a mic. Then he made this strange drumstick, I think it's called the loon drumstick. It curled, sort of like a lacrosse stick. It's the loon; it plays softer. But the drum was really booming all over the house. So he had to have his voice amplified, and so he got his mic.

The songs were never these pow-wow vocables. Mishoomis's songs were about mink, otters, moose, rabbits. When the boys started with pow-wows, Mishoomis went along. But the songs he sang were not the dancing kind. They were a celebration of life and animals, lakes, and rivers.

My younger cousin Patrick liked to learn from Mishoomis, and then he went to Thunder Bay to learn more songs. He came back with all these *hey-yeh, way-yeh* vocables. That puzzled my grandfather for awhile. He said, "What's this *wey-yah, hey-yah?*" He was waiting to hear a story. "This is how you do it," Mishoomis said. "Never mind your *wey-yah, hey-yahs.*" Then he would turn up his amplifier and start singing. "There's a story, a real ballad, you know?"

Mishoomis amplified everything. I remember Ambrose (his son) would then come in half cut and plug in his guitar. Boy! That was loud. I would just sit there, but Patrick wanted to sing, and Mishoomis wanted to sing, and Uncle Ambrose, well he's half cut. One time we were doing that and my sister Veronica walks in. She was Pentecostal, total, and she says, "No, no, this is it, I'm going to sing my songs now." And she started singing these spiritual songs. Everybody took off. I didn't want to stick around and hear that. What are these songs about praising the Lord? But my sister was sobered up, because of this experience, I think, with this church. She was the first to recover from alcoholism, drug addiction. Straight, but very religious. So when she saw that amplifier. . . . Well, everybody had their song.

That amplifier went everywhere with Mishoomis. But when I was up around the village some people were making fun of him. Or were ashamed; I heard some people say something about "little drummer boy." See, that's how colonized we were at that time.

Thankfully there was a younger generation like Patrick and Jimmy. That's when we accepted this *wey-yah, hey-yah*—"Okay, that's how it's done?" And when Jimmy was dancing, boy, he looked really regal.

The Catholic church started inviting us. The priest there was really open minded. "Let's ask our brothers and sisters," he'd say, and he opened the church basement there in Geraldton. That's how that pow-wow slowly evolved out of Geraldton. Then when you did something like that, Longlac and Aroland came and listened. Now I hear there's drum groups out of Longlac, Aroland, and Nipigon.

I've gone to a couple of pow-wows; maybe next year I'll go to more. I don't know. It would have been nice to jam with my grandfather. I think I could improvise a mink song if I wanted. It's in my head; I can see the mink by the shoreline, I can see cedar branches and mink.

These songs live on because our language is musical. I think that's why Mishoomis was a bit upset about vocables; he wanted words sung. Anishinaabemowin. Negamowin. This "mowin." Mowin means to weep. Negam means call and response. Heart and soul, and weeping.

That's why I'm practising this finger-style guitar playing, you know, these soft sounds. That's his influence on me. You can make this big grandfather drum, but if you want to make it tell a story—well, it's softer than your regular honour beat.

That's all I know about Grandfather's approach: storytelling through the drum.

Jingle Dancer

It is you I find
Exquisite.
If I fall behind,
your sunlit
jingles can
convalesce
the broken span
between us.

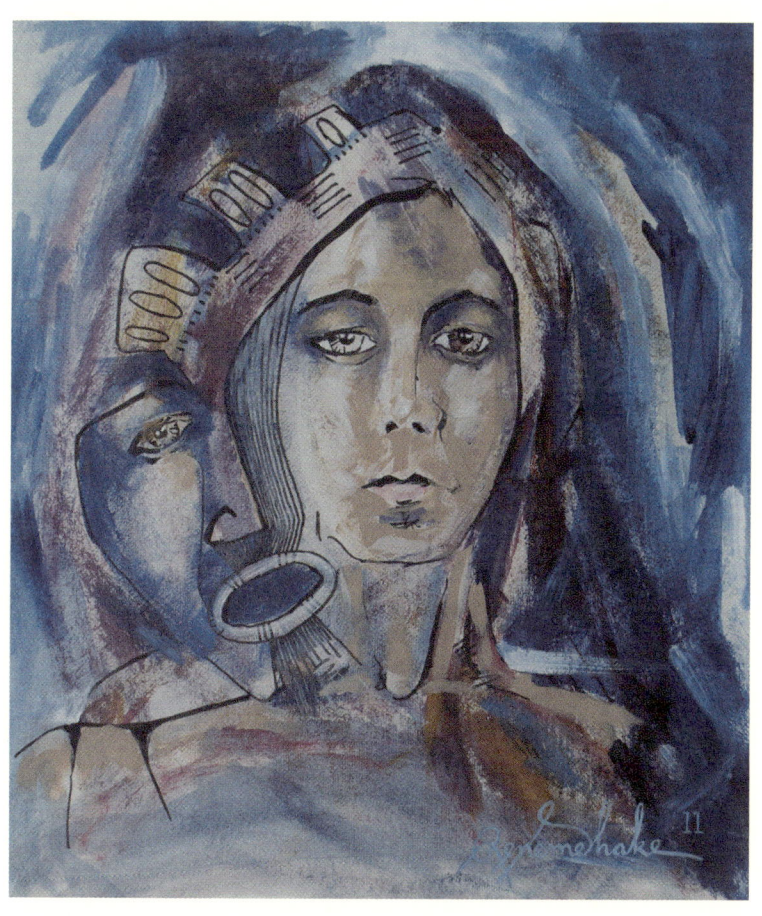

Nagamowin, Sing, 2011, acrylic on paper, 35.6 x 43.2 cm.

Nagamowin,
Sing

Nagam (sing or call); mow (weep); win (state).
   There is mow or weeping in the vocal tone. Blues, anyone?

Round Dance

There was a lot of music in my family. There was Uncle Cashimere—
he was Uncle Ambrose's brother—and he was multi-instrumental.
When I was a small guy he played this huge accordion and it scared
the shit out of me. I thought it was going to swallow me, so I never
went back there! But as a youth I would jam with Uncle Cashimere,
who played guitar, accordion, harmonica, and the fiddle too. Everyone in my family played, all my cousins. Even my dad told me he
played guitar, but when he got married he stopped. "I got your mum,"
he says. "Why should I play guitar?"

It was Uncle Ambrose who taught me how to play harmonica
and guitar. I loved the harmonica because I could carry it wherever
I went—just put it in my pocket. And sometimes there were beautiful tin boxes from my grandfather's store that you could drum on.
Later, when I was a young adult, I bought my own guitars, but I went
through so many because I'd smash them. I'd keep a guitar maybe two
weeks and I'd smash it, always in anger about certain things. Then I'd
buy another one. I did that to my paintings too—I'd finish one and
then take a knife to it. Lose it. Then start another one. But I never
destroyed my harmonicas.

I had another uncle, Emery Gagnon. He was the guy that started
the square dances that my grandfather had in his pool hall. They
would take the tables away and everybody danced. In my earliest times
I remember them doing it every Saturday night. Of course my grandfather was there; he had a little booth where he sold drinks and chips
and chocolates. I guess they had booze too—I don't know—but there

were no fights. I think there were enough grannies around to keep things in order.

It was in my grandfather's pool hall that Uncle Ambrose learned to call. It was his specialty in the community and he loved it: "Promenade her around the hall." "Tap yer leg down." "Swing to the west!"—*Okay, where's the west?*

It was kind of subversive; the government and the church said we weren't supposed to do pow-wows any more. The music died. That's why there were no drums, no flutes, no rattles, no shakers, no pow-wow, no dancing. The only way you get around that is call it a square dance. To us it was a big round dance.

Those dances stopped when we were teenagers. We were not interested in square dancing, but we did have a teen dance every Saturday. We paid a quarter—we saved up for that. Nobody drank at that time. But when we started drinking we dropped everything; no more dances, no more nothing, just straight partying. It didn't mean anything.

I think alcohol destroyed everything. Now there's some in my generation that have quit drinking. I think that's the day my grandfather was looking towards. One day the kids will sober up or straighten out and keep our culture alive.

My Poem Cries

for Stanley J. Meshake, 1952–2016

My poem cries,
my garden plant dies.
The flowerbed
not far from your eyes.
Do not look upon my dying
as a wet plant drying
in the light of stars.
I gave you joy at my birth
I gave you love, hope, and faith.
Why can't you celebrate too?
When my life is through
do not go fearing the night.
Turn to face our Creator's might
in the land of musical grace,
and me—to play the bass.

Validation as a Writer

I wouldn't have the courage to write this book if it weren't for the Banff Centre.

Before Banff, I was writing a one-act play. I soon discovered that other characters appeared out of nowhere in the scenes and disrupted the whole process, and I found myself giving up.

Then one day as I was cruising the web I came upon a call for Aboriginal storytellers for a scriptwriting workshop in Banff. Since I was writing a play, I applied—but soon forgot about it.

It was suppertime a few months later when I got this call. I thought it was telemarketers and I was going to let them have it. The voice on the line said, "Congratulations!" And I thought to myself *they always say that*. But then the person said, "You may board Air Canada to Calgary, Alberta, and we'll pick you up and take you to the Banff Centre." I don't remember the rest.

The Banff people asked for the rest of the ten pages of the play that I had begun. What ten pages? I frantically scanned my hard drive for the files. I don't know where they are! But in spite of this I got to Banff.

Then it happened. The director of *North of 60* television series said, "I see a writer, here," as he was reading my script. Then the producer of *North of 60* said, "I see a writer, too." During that whole workshop—*I see a writer* is all I heard.

During the break, I hiked up the elk and deer trails on the mountain. I took a deep breath, closed my eyes and reached back to the time I was a little boy sitting at his desk at McIntosh Indian residential school. He had just been sexually assaulted, and his dreams were crushed. I touched his small shoulders and said, "Come with me. We're going to write and write and write!"

We wrote our first poem together and it said this:

The Mountain of God

This Anishinaabe
got no more land to give.
I leave you no offering like before.
It is you who gave to me.
You offered me your willow branches
on the slopes
to help me come down the mountain,
and I fell no more.

That little boy and I gave our first spoken word performance over the telephone that night from the Banff Centre, to my dear wife, Joan.

And so the inner child in me earned his validation as a writer.

Inaabiiginan, String

Inaabiig (string); iginan (a certain way).

I had a friend named Luke in residential school—I think he was from Ogoki, or one of the fly-in reserves. And his family used to use string as a form of writing.

One time I saw him get a letter and as he opened up the envelope I could see he was really happy. He pulled out a string. That was the only thing there, and I started laughing. I asked him, "What is that? What do you need a string for?"

He started reading the strings, and he said to me, "This is how tall my little brother is now." The string told the rest of story.

I can just see the nuns trying to figure that out. They used to censor our mail. I can see them opening up his mail, and saying, "Oh, it's just a bunch of string . . . Give it to him."

So Luke read inaabiiginan in secret. There might have been knots all over it, but all he told me was, "This is how tall he is." That's all he told me. Subversive as he was!

Wanibii'ige,
Writing Error

Wani (lose); bi'ige (inscribe or write).

Anishinaabeg knew about wanibii'ige because they had a form of writing: birchbark scrolls, pictographs, and petroglyphs. Syllabics were developed by James Evans (1801–1846)—a missionary, and that's the reason I do not write in syllabics. Where are the birchbark scrolls? Alternatively, I am a person of digital scrolls, Weshibiiged.

Jiibik,
PhD

Elder within the Rez
tutors O'jiibik in the Language Ways.
Linguist bereft of Rez
honours O'jiibik with a PhD and says,
"The Linguist has sprung
O'jiibik from his taboo
and heal his Ojibwe tongue,"
that Linguist cut-off long ago.

Gagansoma, Counsel

Gagans (push); soma (speak to inform).

Spoken words that inspire, elevate, enlighten, and heal push you into greater self-confidence and build character.

Notification Letter

Tick-tock tick-tock
tolls the mantel clock,
timing me to mock
my patience. I unlock
my fingers to peel
my mail and seal,
to read, with zeal
"I am pleased," to which I kneel.

Quest for Words

Sometimes I think my whole life is a vision quest, and it moves around with me. Like when Joan and I went to Ireland. My introduction to this crazy world of the quest was a big key chain at the hotel when we arrived.

It had a big heavy metal ball on the end—it looked like a weapon. You could have knocked somebody out with it! I put it in the keyhole and the door wouldn't open—it was just stuck, and I was all jet-lagged with no patience at all. So I was starting to curse and felt like giving up, but then I just pushed the doorknob straight ahead and without even turning the key it opened! I was trying to figure out *what's going on here?* Maybe you only have to nudge the Irish people very gently to open the door of stories? Then they'll give you a story, just like every cab driver eventually did as we travelled around Dublin.

So the stories are part of the quest. That's what Nagweidisowin means: vision quest. Nagwe is things appear, and you appear with them. Nagwe is to take care of, to nourish, even yourself. Idiso is yourself—the self begins with you. Sowin is the action and the state. You put these three together and you get this vision quest. You're seeking, and when you seek, that vision takes care of you.

That first day I arrived in Ireland, while I was resting in a semi-sleep, I heard these voices saying, "Don't ever be afraid of your words."

Your words.

So, when I came back to Canada, I started writing poetry again. I feel freer now than I ever was with writing.

When we first met, Joan didn't know I was fluent in my language because I hardly ever talked to her in Ojibwe. Now I speak to her in

Ojibwe, and I speak to anyone in Ojibwe. When I'm performing I use it. But when you are in Indian residential school you are told so much about the inferiority of your language you think that it's irrelevant. Even within the Anishinaabe community at day school I was made fun of by other students because I spoke the Aroland dialect, and of course the nuns didn't want me to speak that language. So then you start to disrespect your own mother—that's your mom, the language—or your grandmother.

That internal suppression of the language even affected how I used English, and I could never write the way I wanted to. Words were so hidden, packed away somewhere in my soul. The only words I felt very comfortable with were the swear words, you know, "fuck you." Every sentence was "fuck you, fuck this, fuck that." I was afraid of using something that was meaningful, beautiful, encouraging, or nourishing. I couldn't even compliment someone.

Fear of words.

So you never know what the Irish and their land did to me. And when the spirits of their ancestors told me, "Don't be afraid of your words,"—man, now I'm not.

PART SEVEN

Migisiwiganj
Stories of Regeneration

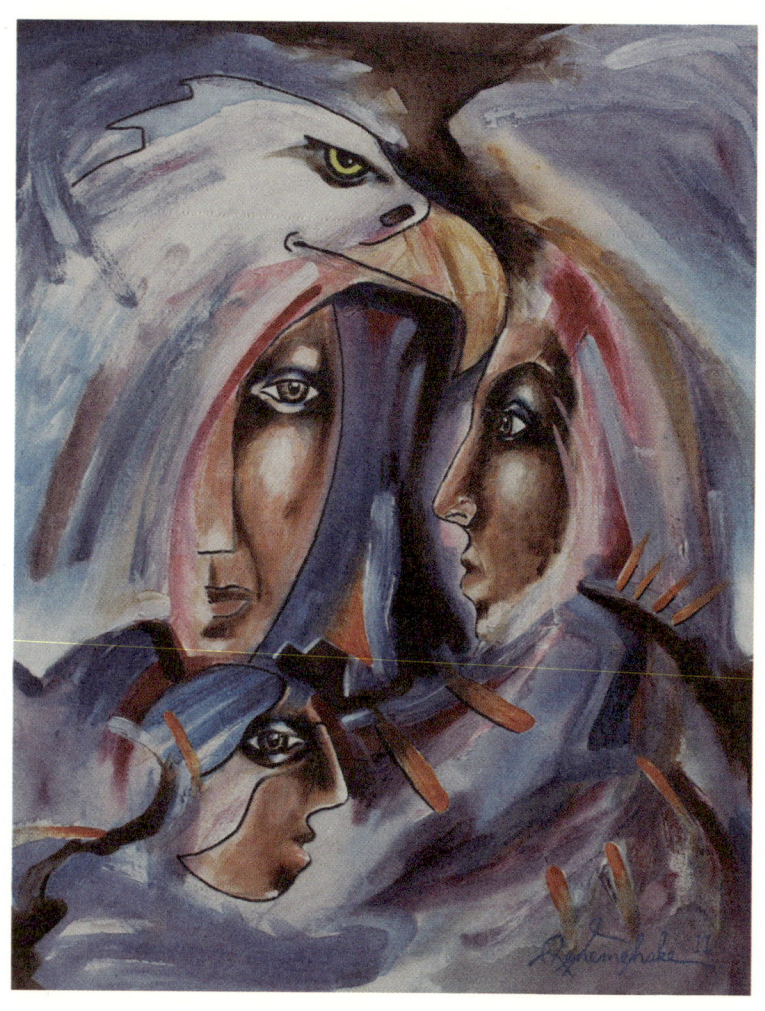

Migisiwiganj, 2011, acrylic on canvas, 40.6 x 50.8 cm.

Migisiwiganj

Migisi (Eagle); wi (possessive); ganj (claw).

Wadikwaning apane migiswiganj gishi aia. Imandi migisi ogiki-
noamaawag odooshianak jinandawenjigewad. Giishka'aakweg
waawiidamaagewag Bimaadjitamasowin. Megwa gi babitonawadj
waawiidamaagewin, ga ishi giishka'igadegin odikwanan. Kawiin dash
migisiwiganj gi banaadisinoon.

Oshki mitig gi kitigazo dash, mi imandi migisiwiganj miinwa gi
onigiigomaged.

The same eagle's claw had always held the same perch, year after
year. From its position, the eagle taught his young family how to skill-
fully use their claws to catch food. Then came the loggers promising
a gourmet feast for all. While the eagles waited for the promise, they
lost their perch to clear-cutting. But the eagle's claw has not been lost.

A new tree has been planted on which the eagle's claw will
perch once again.

Grandmother Pipe

There is a spiritual world of women with lots of room for mystery; even Anishinaabeg had mermaids. But what I've seen is Grandmother Pipe.

She came one morning when my grandmother and I were visiting a relation along the CNR tracks. CNR had these sections and each section had a foreman with a house. These CNR foremen often married Indian women, some of whom were our aunts. So my grandmother and I went visiting our relative who lived at this beautiful big log house out in the bush.

One morning I woke to hear them saying, "Wegonesh indawenda-mon? Angodjiishan oma . . . angodjiishan oma!" They had been busy washing dishes, and suddenly were standing by the doorway. I saw them looking out, calling, "Angodjiishan." To paraphrase, that means, "Go away from here" and "What do you want?"

I got curious. I thought, *Who are they talking to anyways? Is there a big bull moose out there by the door?* I ran to them and then I saw this apparition in the treetop of a big spruce; a woman, just glowing and flowing. It felt natural, just like another grandmother, so I wasn't scared. But my grandmother said, "Bego ginwensh gana wahamaken. Gamadjiinig." She was telling me, "Don't look at her for too long. She will take you away." Gamadjiinig—that means she's going to take you away if you look too long. But only if you stare at her.

I ran outside, but I listened to my grandmother's words. I went to the bedrock at the foot of the tree and started piling little rocks in circles, pretending this was a fort and that I was battling enemies outside the

240

circle. Inside the circle was my family and I was protecting them. As the enemies came at us, I piled my little rocks higher and higher.

Every now and then I'd peek up at this tree and I would see her there. She was like a light but dressed in these robes—a regalia that was translucent, the colour of blue ice. Her regalia sparkled in the sun and the fabric sounded like crystals. That's quite a fabric, to ring like that; to chime as she moves and breathes. It's like icicles in the spring-time smashing against each other; a really natural sound, this beautiful soft music. I hear it sometimes if I go near the lake. When I hear the ice moving, I think she's there somewhere.

I think that was godjiewisiwin for me. I was being tested about obedience; whether I was going to obey my grandmother or the Grandmother Pipe. I kept on playing, looking down, and when I eventually looked up again she was gone.

The grandmothers knew something about it, but they never told me. I guess these things happened in the past—kids go missing and never come back. "Giwanishin" means they must have been lost or taken away by spirits. Whether these spirits are good or bad, we don't know.

For the longest time that troubled me because I didn't know what it was all about. But when I started sobering up in Pedahbun Lodge I described it to an Elder. After listening carefully, she told me, "That's Grandmother Pipe; the tree is the stem and that little fort you built was the bowl. It's made of rock." Then I saw it immediately, and now every tree I see reminds me of that image.

I've heard other stories about Buffalo Calf Woman, who walked out of the mist and gave the sacred bundle when the people were starving and had started to disrespect the earth. That sounds like Grandmother Pipe too, and maybe that's the message. And we can still find Grandmother Pipe at the places we build for her.

Anishinaabe Sentence

Secluded and nowhere to go.
In a world of no birthdays
yet their blossoms blow,
born of budding praise.
Does anyone know?
Small-Feet wander amiss
on the land giving no way home.
Who will cross the abyss?
To regale us with the plume,
to burn us awake with a kiss.

Bidaabaan,
Dawn

Bida (approaching); da (home); baan (past).

Nookomis, you once told me that dawn, bidaaban in our language, contains future, present, and past. Bidaaban. The light of dawn approaches, stays with you, and then leaves you!

Chibekana,
Milky Way

Chibe (ghost or spirit); kana (trail).

The Milky Way is the Ghost Trail of the Anishinaabeg. I shall journey there with all my relations when I make a Grand Entry into the spirit world.

Beginnings

I can still remember what my son looked like when he was first born. I saw a very ancient face; I saw my grandfather, because his face showed a lot of the past—threw me right back there. I guess sometimes when people are born we see ancient faces or spirits in this beautiful bundle of life.

There was no turning back once my son arrived. It was a rite of passage.

In the years that have passed, I have felt truly blessed to have dealt with some of the trauma of my earlier life. I didn't want him to have this Indian residential school legacy—he doesn't need all that weight that I carried around for decades. That's why I hope that other fathers and mothers can deal with IRS legacies too. We have better challenges to meet: we can be creative, write books, change the story.

We talk about reclamation of land and stuff; all this reclaiming is more than just land. It's life, it's reclaiming your gifts. That's the message I got from my son, and it sealed a door. I realized that what I have to do in life is return to the past, because there's a lot of power there.

Aanike-Bimadisiwin, Generation

Aanik (arm); nike (in arm); bimaadisiw (life); win (state).

Aanike-bimadiwisin describes a generation living arm in arm. When one member succeeds, all succeed.

Box Drum

I bought a cajon. As I sat there slapping and keeping in time with the melody in my head, it took me back to a winter in northwestern Ontario. I was visiting my uncle Cashimere. As he was playing his fiddle, I sat listening on a soft-drink wooden packing crate. Intuitively, I began drumming the crate. We jammed. We had a big, jig-time groove going. We even took our concert to my grandmother's house and soon the whole family gathered and tapped their legs down.

I found this memory to be priceless. It was the only time that my grandmother and family came close to a pow-wow. There was no such thing as a pow-wow in the sixties. No drum. Yet drumming came naturally to me. Ergo, my box drum: a packing crate from my grandfather's general store.

Biiwideg, Pyre

Stars like birds,
preening on limbless blackening hills
flicker dark words
to announce the Biiwideg wills.
The Ojibwe gypsy fire
and the lights upon the hills
join the Biiwideg pyre
with songs and thrills.
Show Biiwideg medicines
respect, or you will never know
what makes a woman of means
drum with hope for tomorrow.
Nookomis victory and fire
blaze on limbless blackening hills,
stoke the Biiwideg pyre
with songs and thrills.

Piano Lessons

I had two chances at taking piano lessons when I was a kid. First, when I was in grade two and I met this French "fille" taking piano lessons from a nun at the school on my rez. When we were on the porch we could hear her. Then she would get picked up by her parents and away they went.

I wanted to play piano too, but grandmother couldn't pay for the lessons. I took consolation by listening to the music at church and concerts.

Another chance came when I was in grade five at the McIntosh Indian Residential School. I think Canada really lost out on arts and culture, because a lot of us had talent there. I remember every Christmas they held a recital. The kids went up on stage and played their little piece. There were poets and storytellers too—we were all talented people. But what happened was Indian residential school really derailed everything.

At McIntosh I used to hear other kids practising their pieces downstairs. I really wanted to learn to read and write music and I was just about ready to ask my teacher if I could play piano too. But something happened that crushed my musical ambitions. I was sexually assaulted! That's when I stopped illustrating and writing stories and poems, and I began to believe that I was unworthy to make music.

I was deaf and mute for almost seventy years. But when I found my piano teacher at the age of sixty-eight I was thunderstruck! I found my voice! And that voice took me back to the Anishinaabe boy learning to read and write English by the coal oil lamp. Now the boy had become an Anishinaabe man learning to read and write music by the computer screen.

Akiwensi,
Old Man

Akiw (I am earth); wensi (way of; return or come again).

Western society is always talking about going to heaven, but the word Akiwensi (old man) implies that as you get older you are bending closer to the earth. You are returning to dust; giving life to trees, to worms—everything. As that life-giving force that travels everywhere, you become one with the earth and the air.

I feel the thunder from the ground up these days! I am Akiwensi. It's destruction and renewal. I think it also means to return to the old ways. I'm on that same journey.

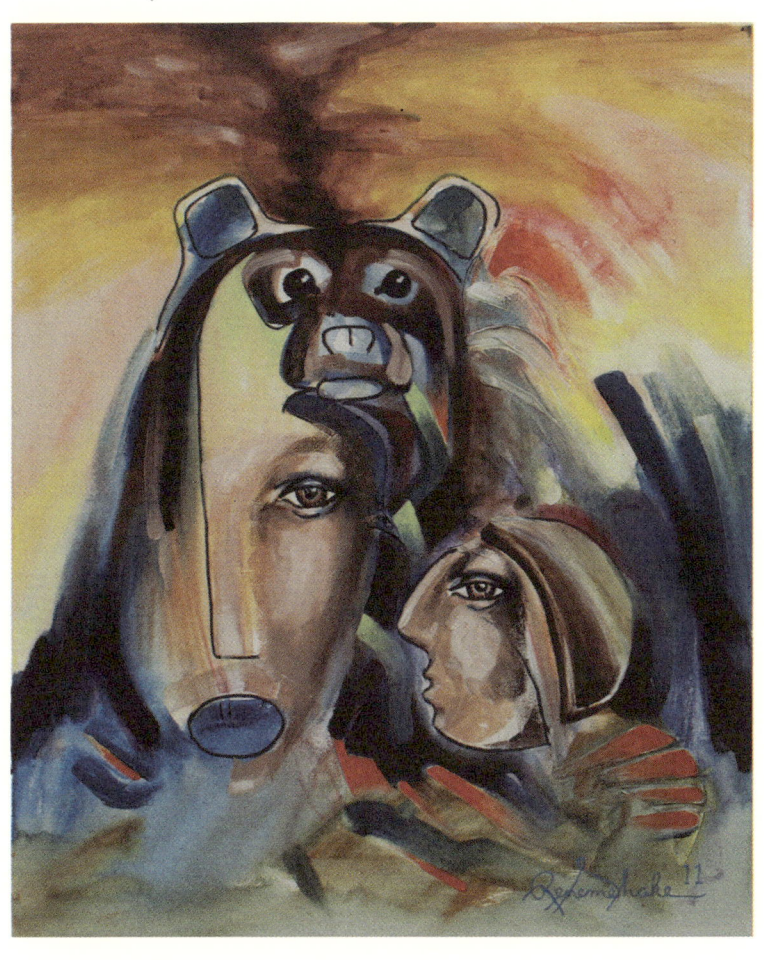

Old Man Makwa 1, 2011, acrylic on canvas, 40.6 x 50.8 cm.

We Are Still Here

Nidjaaniss
Dangerous!
It's all right if we make
arts and crafts.
It's not all right if we partake
when songend da mowin staffs
self-determination.
The power of spirit,
Manidoo wisi win.
Steep in the gift,
too deep to keep in
a reservation.
Nidjaaniss
Dangerous!
Mother our blood and bone.
Gather to light
the sober wiing gashk koon.
Sweet grass bright
with transformation.
Reconciliation then
will see the first glint
of bon nend da mowin,
fire and flint.
Life is sincere
in the Ojibwe camp, and oh!
We are still here!
Awa'si aginz zo!

Chibegamig, Graveyard

Chibai (ghost or spirit); gamig (lodge).

Traditionally a grandparent would prepare to enter the spirit world by building himself/herself a chibegaming (ghost lodge) to die. He/she offered his/her flesh to the animals to be eaten, in return for the meat that he/she took from them. No one was permitted to come near the chibegaming ever! This is one aspect of Anishinaabe spirituality.

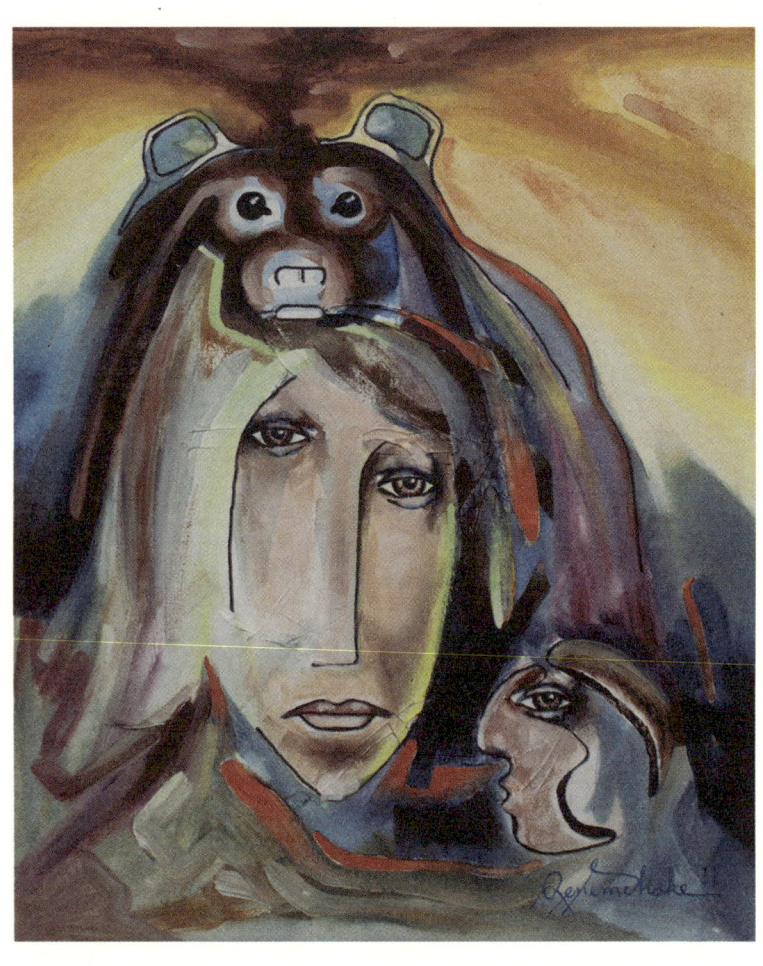

Old Man Makwa 2, 2011, acrylic on canvas, 40.6 x 50.8 cm.

Bear Spirit Manidowiwin

In one of my art workshops a student asked me about the bear spirit. I told her about the time Nookomis and I went blueberry picking.

I was nine. Nookomis told me to stay and pick blueberries while she walked away, disappearing over the hill. It was reassuring when her shadow reappeared, and I began picking blueberries again with delight. But I wanted to know why my grandmother had left me to go over that hill, and so I made my way up to have a peek. There I saw a startled bear cub running away from me.

I later learned that Nookomis and Makwa (bear) had negotiated an agreement so that we could pick blueberries on the north end of the blueberry patch while they had the south side. That ridge formed the boundaries of the blueberry glade.

There was another example regarding the boundaries between Nookomis and Makwa. It involved an annual tradition where every family went down the river to the rapids for whitefish spawning time. All of our families used to camp on one side of the spawning grounds. No one camped on the other side of the rapids. The other side was for Makwa and other animals to feast on the whitefish.

I remember the smell of smoked fish in the evenings. I remember the mutual respect and sharing between the bears and Anishinaabeg families of that sacred land. We may have lost much of those times, but the bear spirit of sharing, manidowiwin, was part of that workshop with my student.

Belonging

I turned 70 this year and I'm naming it my golden years. Whoever is 70 out there, I'd like to encourage you to feel it too—this is "the new 70!"—and there are choices. You can become bitter with life, or you can feel that self-determination. For me, it's wide open now: I now have a new sense of awe, for the world is still wondrous, and it's full of better angels. Like our Canadian allies—they're the better angels, willing to work with me in academia, the art world—wherever. So that's where I fit in now. I find a lot of inspiration in my life as a self-employed artist. It's a place of belonging, as I've never met a closed artist in my life!

In this technological age there are new ways of belonging too. I'll give an example. One day, I was feeling agitated as I was sitting around alone in the house. Joan was away, it was winter, and it was bitterly cold. Then I saw a story on Facebook about one of my relatives who went out late and by the time he walked home, he had a sheepish grin of a grimace, just frozen on his face! So I posted this story on Facebook:

> *Was feelin' anxious, eh? Bein' it's a brrrr kind of cold,*
> *I stepped outside and let the chill freeze a great, big smile on*
> *my face. Then, I goes downtown and people thought that I was*
> *a smilin' and theys smiled back at me. Came back home just in*
> *time for my frozen smile to thaw out! Now, I'm laughin' all by*
> *myself and not feelin' anxious anymore! Ahh ha ha ha!*

It made me realize that I have an online community now and that there are many ways of connecting in the new 70.

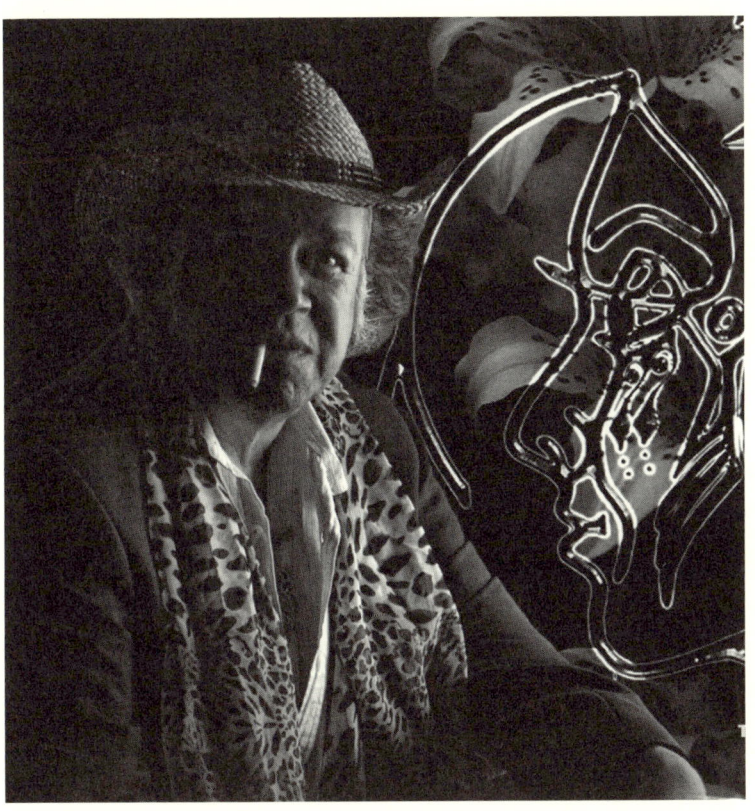

Rene hamming it up as Keith Richards, in "The New 70!" (Note: Rene doesn't smoke; for performance fun only). Photo by Joan Bruder.

That post also shows that I have a sense of belonging in my new odena (home) and heart community, the city of Guelph. I felt this one day when I went downtown and saw a man lying on the street near the steps of one of the churches. He had bumped his head and there was blood coming out of his skull. I don't know what happened, but then I saw a lot of people getting blankets out of their cars, covering him, trying to keep him warm. I said, "Yeah, that's my community!" And then there was another guy on his cell phone, calling the ambulance. I said, "Yeah, yeah, this is the community I belong in." I felt safe because we have people in this city doing that. I thought, *If I fell and had a concussion like that, I'm sure these people would be around.* That is my city; that is my community. And as I walked home thinking about these things, one of my neighbours said, "Hello Rene, how are you?" They mentioned my name and asked how I am. So that is a sense of belonging; of being accepted. I feel most alive and grateful.

Sometimes I see people walking around like they're trudging— like they're carrying a big weight. I must have walked like that on the street, unless I was drunk. I do still have these milder depressions, but they're not heavy, they're not weighing me down. I ride them out now with prayer, and by keeping active, keeping creative. I keep taking these online workshops, things like Photoshop, and then I get that sense of accomplishment that makes me proud, happy that I learned something. I also know that I have to be kind and honest with Rene. They say with addictions you have to have rigorous honesty. I can't drink. I'm an alcoholic. I'm starting to express that when I see candies. *No Rene, you're a diabetic.* I tell people that. They respect that.

I take compliments now too. I never accepted compliments before in my life because I felt like I didn't deserve anything positive. I'd squirm inside if somebody said nice things to me. But if you swore at me and cursed me, I would be fine with that; I agreed with that.

So that's the life, accepting compliments. Learning to make real decisions. And when I make them, I'm not as stressed out.

In this vision quest of life, I've had lots of better angels and mentors along the way. Early on, there were also a lot of people that said, "You can't do this; you can't do that," but I no longer meet those ones. More often I meet people now that say, "Go for it, man!"

Miskwabikisi, Blood Moon

Miskwa (blood); wabik (metal); kisi (moonlight).

The blood moon enlightens us about the wabik (iron) in our blood. But there is also wabi (to see). We will see a time of great change when there are four blood moons. For four is a sacred number among our Anishinaabeg nation! Miskwabikisi has much to tell us about self-examination and to transfer that wisdom to our children.

The Ceremony
of Homecoming

I have only gone back to my home communities of Aroland and Longlac a few times since my dad died. We went as a family when my son
was about ten, and then in 2015 I went with Joan and our friend Kim
as part of the research for this book. I had also long wanted to do a
ceremony for Nookomis, giving us another reason to go.

It was a great visit with family and friends, and I made some discov-
eries about relatives that I hadn't known. But it was also hard to go
back. There was one incident where we went to a community feast
in Aroland, and in the midst of handing out prizes, one of the orga-
nizers made the loud point that the prizes were "for band members
only." My maternal grandmother had been a Long Lake band member,
but my paternal grandfather was from Aroland, and I had always
spent time in both. Now there I was, feeling unrecognized, which
is also how I felt upon coming home from Indian residential school.
So sometimes I think band membership separates us—from friends,
families, land, sky, and water. Fortunately, my cousins were more
welcoming, acknowledging that I am now among the oldest in the
Mishakegizhig family and therefore have responsibilities toward the
younger generations.

I got to see some of my Elders while I was there. Sadly, one of oldest
martriachs, my aunt Christine, was in the hospital in her final days.
When I went to see her I held her hand and felt how strong she was.
All she said to me was, "Menagowabamin," which means "I'll see you

again." It stuck with me all that night; I was wondering if she meant the traditional "I'll see you on the other side," the spirit world.

The next day I was out walking on the shoreline and I saw a piece of driftwood that looked like a sword. It was silvery and coming out of the water in such a way that it looked like the water was holding it. When I took pictures, I saw battle scars on it. I thought about my aunt, who went through a lot of pain and suffering but also had many victories on the way. Like many of those old matriarchs, she was a real battle woman. I picked up that driftwood, and when I held the blade it felt the same as when I was holding her hand. Bone and wood.

On our fourth day, it was time to pay my respects to my Nookomis. Joan, Kim, and I packed into my cousin's truck and the four of us drove from Longlac out to the territory of Pagwashing. *Pagwashing;* that's real mushgeegik, the real medicine, where Nookomis raised me. There aren't any houses there anymore, as they were burned down in the 1950s, but we found the railroad tracks and from there started to look for ways to make our way into the creek.

The first place we stopped was alongside the highway. We spotted a pathway into the bush and were making our way there when all of a sudden this white guy appeared in "camo" gear and an orange safety vest. We remembered being told that it was bear hunting season, and some of these guys like to hunt with crossbows.

We peered in behind him and could see that he had a little camouflage tent and had hung a pail of bear bait on a tree in the distance. I guess he waited there all day, watching for a bear from his tent. I could just imagine that bear in the woods watching *him*, waiting until he left for lunch and then ripping that pail right off the tree! We laughed about it later, remembering how this guy had warned us not to go any further: "Let me kill the bear first, then you guys can come back." Even though my cousin and I told him we grew up in that bush, he seemed to think he needed to make it safe for us. I should have told him, "You're hunting a spirit, guy. You get out of here, not us."

This encounter directed us to drive further along. We went down a side road and knew it was the right way when we saw all this beautiful medicine, and a red fox greeted us. We got out and my cousin and

I made a trail through the bush. The women, the ishkwe, the fire came after. It was so good to have the Lifegivers with us, and before long we found those waters we had used to make rabbit stew, tea—everything! It was that creek that had sustained our community and our spirit. People had warned us that it was dangerous with the bear hunters moving around in there, but I didn't care about arrows flying through. I just thought, I've got to do this ceremony, one way or another. *Even if I die doing it, I'll do it.* I wanted to protect the bear too! So I talked to him in my prayers, "Be careful; stay out in the bush."

I could feel that my grandmother was still strong there; stronger than ever. I felt protected. Then we took out the kerchiefs we had brought and hung them in the trees, working in a beautiful balance, as two men and two women. The four elements were present: the water of the creek, the fire of the women, the air, cleansed by the wind blowing through the young pines, and the earth.

After we were done, I had the feeling that it was now Gibamaik, a spirit place, a sacred place. We left with strength and courage and a memory, peace.

I think it is so vital to pass ceremonies like this down to the young ones so they won't feel lost, adrift, or without love. There's no script for what we did; I think ceremonies like this are constantly being rein-vented according to need and according to the guidance that you get. But I also had the feeling that some ceremonies you can't gather and take home with you. You can't even go back there. That's the one we had. So when we left, I gave my cousin the driftwood sword that I had found, that day my aunt was dying. I think maybe it was for him to do his own ceremony somewhere else.

On our last night of that trip, it was a September blood moon. We had some family come out to visit in the little cabin we had rented, and when my niece went outside to smoke a cigarette in the misty rain, it reminded me of the time my grandmother had put up a sweat lodge. I had only ever witnessed Nookomis doing this once; she was inside and had given my aunt Christine a cigarette to smoke outside the lodge while they prayed together. I felt like we were doing the same thing; healing and cleansing, some sixty years later. When I went outside to

be with my niece I felt the rain on my face like never before. I felt a
baby, a young man and family standing next to me, and realized I am
the oldest man in my family now.

We feasted that night on moose, rice, and a local speciality, "dirty
porridge"—oatmeal made with gravy. There was a lot of laughter, and
a lot of stories. My niece had brought her two-year-old granddaugh-
ter, who was a bundle of energy and life and curiosity. That baby had
dark, dark eyes, just like the sky outside. They were tracking me, speaking to me, just like the rain. I saw hope and recorded these thoughts:

> *Brothers and sisters, the blood moon is going to rise. I don't know yet
> what is going to happen, but I think it's going to be love, hope, faith, a
> renewed bimadowissin. Be prepared, fathers and mothers, to explain
> our ancestors, our history, our family staffs. Be prepared because our
> children are learning to swim like the beaver, like the muskrats on this
> beautiful shoreline of our ancestors' history.*

It was on that trip, on those original shorelines, that I saw logs
that looked like bones sticking out. I saw grass and young pine trees,
and way back, the clear-cut. I also saw this spruce tree growing on
the sand, and I thought that in spite of all the erosion of our culture,
there's something growing.

This growth goes back to the beginning. I think my umbilical cord
is buried in Pagwashing, and that is why I'm connected to that land.
So I'll never be far away because my spirit will always be there, in the
air and the earth and the water and the fire of our women.

I am blessed.

Closing Words

I will leave you with this story or dibaadjimowin. Turtle Island, or as Nookomis would call it, "Miniss," The Island, can only be seen in her original language, Anishinaabemowin. If our original language ceases to exist from our communities, the land will cease to exist. All that will be left is pollution and our original language polluted. We'd have no way to define our homelands as minobimadisiwin, the good life, anymore. I have attempted in this book to safeguard Miniss when I've interweaved our Anishinaabemowin in my story. I'd be pleased if even a single Anishinaabe word was included in our future greetings and conversations. In that event, we are all Kino'amaaganak: Disciples of Anishinaabemowin.

Miigwetch, Thank You

Miigwe (to give); wetch (giver).

Miigwetch. It seems to me that the meaning has layers and layers. Miigwe is to give, wetch—who is he? The giver is Gitchi Manido, the Grand Mystery or Creator. You acknowledge the Creator; the final giver. And you are humbled by it.

It's a ceremonial thing. I remember people saying miigwetch when my grandmother would distribute the moose meat. But where does all the moose meat come from? The Giver. Because the person didn't create the moose meat. So we'd better honour the Creator. I think that's what it means. Thanksgiving.

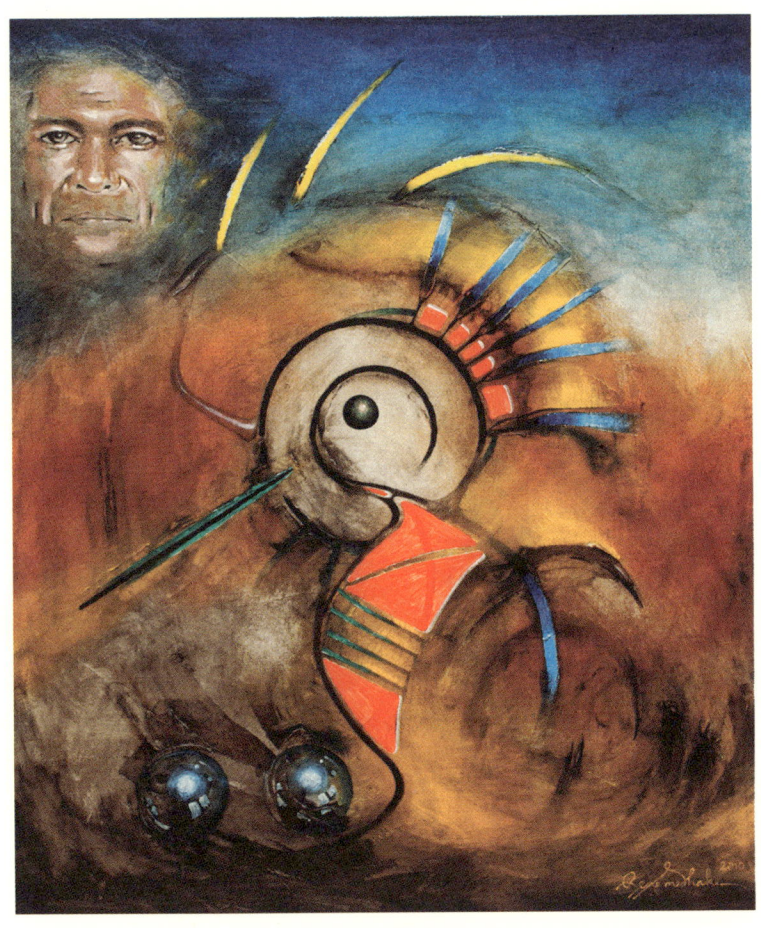

Uncle Biidan, 2011, acrylic on canvas, 76.2 x 91.4 cm.

Epilogue

It's the first day of spring, 2019, and Rene is coming to the University of Guelph to do a "Made in Guelph" language tour of the campus. With the *Injichaag* book done and off to the publishers we have moved on to new projects. For his part, Rene has been busy learning the finer points of his music software and using his "Techno-Elder" skills to build audio-visual word bundles that he shares on Facebook. He has brought his language and composing skills into work with opera singers as they introduce Anishinaabe language and story into new forums. He's recently written and illustrated an Anishinaabe-mowin colouring book that some colleagues and I have incorporated into a local museum exhibition about Indigenous women. He's been fixing up old radios so that we might use them to transmit stories and language lessons from the porch of the grannie's cabin (*Nokum's House*) that we intend to build in the University arboretum. And with others, we are leading a research team that is looking at everyday ways to bring Anishinaabemowin onto the campus.

Our latest project falls within greater efforts across the country to "Indigenize" educational institutions. It's part of an undoing of the devastation wrought by Indian residential schools; one that will require mammoth and prolonged effort as it means shaking the colonial foundations of places like universities. Working with Rene has reminded me of the insidious reach of such places; this came through the first time that Rene and Joan came to visit me in the grand old brick building that houses my office. I found them waiting in the musty entranceway at the bottom of the interior staircase, looking up at the wood banisters that fan out to frame the wainscoted landing.

As we made our way up those stairs toward the stained-glass window that reads "Macdonald Institute, 1903," Rene quipped, "This place reminds me of being in court!"

In the course of our work on the *Injichaag* book, Rene and I have spent years sharing stories and drinking tea in the comfort of his living room, surrounded by art and electronics and musical instruments. Moving forward, we will continue to work as part of the growing community that is shaping and living new Indigenous spaces into being. This involves creating home in new territories, sometimes literally, as in our case Rene and I don't live and work in the homelands of our own people, but in the "Dish with one Spoon" territory, the treaty lands of the Mississaugas. But these are fertile hunting grounds; we have landed where the Haudenosaunee and the Mississaugas once generously envisioned how we might put away sharp utensils to enjoy what the dish has to offer. Within these new lands we also take on new kin, and Rene and I have been building kinship since that day we first spotted each other at the Guelph arts "schmoozefest." The work is transformational, it is ceremony. Our work on *Injichaag* has resulted in Rene naming me (Wakeiabanok) and later adopting me, so now we are growing in new ways as Mishoomis and Odaanis. All of this teaches me that as much as colonization dispossesses Indigenous peoples of land, language and kin, there is a resilience that ensures we find each other and recreate wherever we go. Or as Rene once said, "They can bulldoze our sacred sites but they can't bulldoze the spirit of our ancestors!"

Today, as we get ready to do the language tour, Rene—whom I will henceforth refer to as Mishoomis—sits on the red couch in my university office looking around at the Indigenous art and beadwork that adorn the walls and shelves. His uncle Biidaan looks down protectively over my desk from where he sits in the painting of Pipigwan that hovers above. The eagle feather that Mishoomis Ambrose handed down is resting on the shelves with all my other medicines, ready to offer comfort and vision to students and others that come to visit. There's a framed picture on the windowsill that Joan took of Mishoomis and me posing in front of the "Long Lake No. 58 First

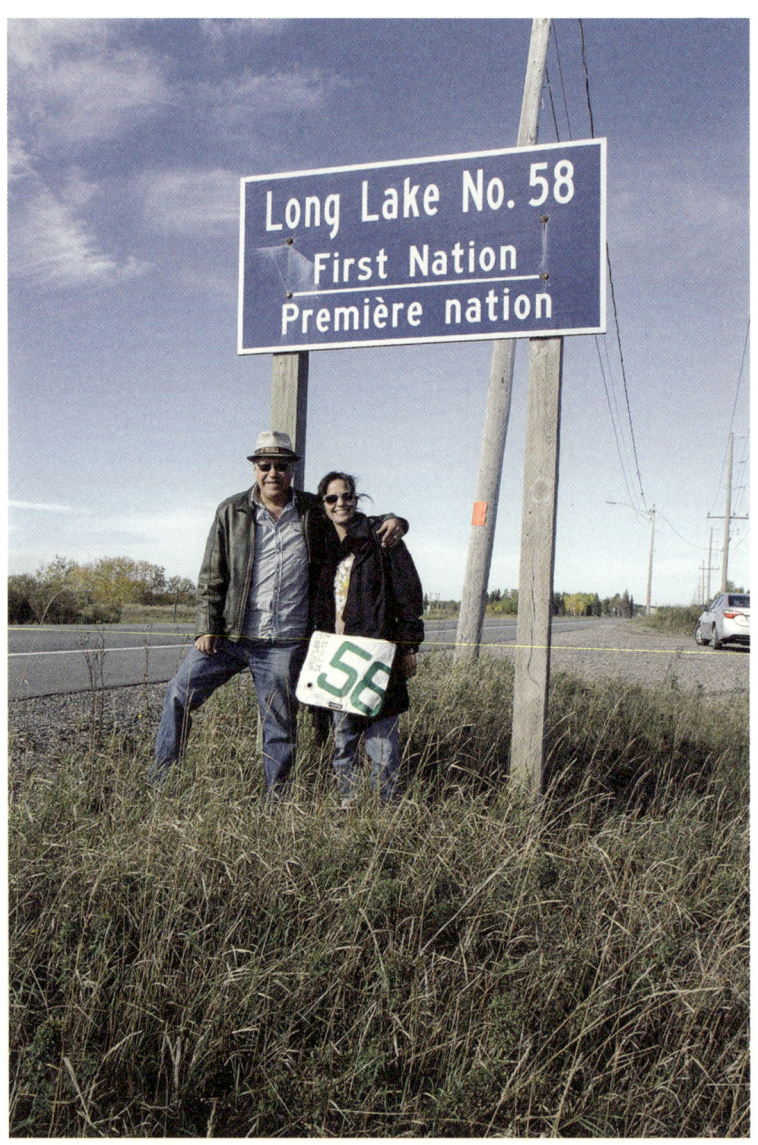

Rene Meshake and Kim Anderson. Photo by Joan Bruder.

Nation" sign; a holding place for the powerful memories of our visit to his homelands.

As he sits there looking about, Mishoomis starts talking about how he was recently meditating on a story he read in the Bible: *The Siege Lifted* (2nd Kings, 7:3). "It's about four lepers," he says, and then he explains that, sitting outside the gates of their city, the lepers decide that if they are going to die anyway, why not go to the enemy's camp? When they go to the enemy's camp, they discover it abandoned and full of riches. "So they go in and start eating and drinking—just partying, putting on the clothes; there's silver, gold . . . ," Mishoomis tells me. "But then they feel bad that they are keeping it to themselves so they go back to find their people to share with them; to bring them into the camp." We laugh when Mishoomis says, "See, we're like those lepers!" And then he says, "We've made it in here, and now we're going to bring our people too."

Our riches are language and story and we have dreamed up the Anishinaabemowin tour idea with colleagues Chelsea Brant, from the University Aboriginal Resource Centre, and Ola Bergier, our post-doctoral language project coordinator. It came to us when we took Mishoomis out for coffee and spent a few hours talking about how we might go about naming and renaming our immediate, everyday environments in Anishinaabemowin. As Mishoomis describes in *Injichaag*, language and story live in places. He reiterated that message to us in the coffee shop, glancing up at the paintings on the wall beside where we are sitting and musing about how he might interpret that café environment through Anishinaabemowin. Amidst uproarious laughter about things like getting an Anishinaabe-talking hamster as our project mascot, we cooked up an idea about doing a "made in Guelph" language tour that would begin with students telling us their stories. Mishoomis would listen and then help students develop personal word bundles. In so doing, we might "Indigenize" the meaning of those places for them, bring it home. "It can be the beginning of a Guelph dialect!" Mishoomis said.

When we start the tour the students don't hesitate to tell us stories about their first impressions of buildings. They talk about when they came to campus for the first time; the excitement and nervousness they felt. They talk about places where they have written exams with large groups of people and the collective nervous energy going in as well as the sense of relief one feels on the way out. Mishoomis listens to the stories and tells his own stories about odena, creating new, breathing places of the heart; mino bimaadiziwin, the good life; kino'amaage, being gifted with direction toward knowledge; and godjiwisiwin, trials. He talks about the word for building or school grounds: kino'amaadii-wigamig, the suffix: gamig, and how it relates to building near gamiing: water, how our peoples often made their lodges near waterways. We talk about the proximity of the two rivers in the community where we live. As we move about the campus, we feel the magic happen through the space that story and language are creating between the students and Mishoomis, between youth and elders. It confirms a place of arrival. We are turning the tea cup right side up again.

Walking back to lunch after the tour, Mishoomis tells me about a dream he had in which he was teaching lots of young people; how he had Joan on one side, and someone on the other side that he didn't know. "Maybe it was you," he says. The next day, he sends an email to me and Ola about his experience:

Thurs/3/21/2019, 12:53pm
Bozho cheers! Indaanis and Ola:
I can't remember a time that I had so
much fun teaching Anishinaabemowin.
Miigwetch apitchi.

I finally figured out what I'll be doing.
I want to collaborate on the work of Indigenizing
the Guelph campus
and grow the language along the Eramosa River.

*I believe our Creator has issued me a challenge — I feel
it in my bones.
I identify with these four lepers.* LOL!
*In our case, we've entered the castle. Now, we wait for
the gates to be open again.
Ahow, minawa apii,
Mishoomis*

As we move on to new projects and new spaces where we find
ourselves, I am mindful of how lucky we are to be alive and doing
this work; mindful of all our relations who didn't make it or who
continue to suffer the most brutal consequences of those systems that
oppress. I am grateful that Mishoomis has told a story of resilience
and survival that gives us hope, while also reminding us that there is
so much work that remains.

And so we'll keep telling.

Or, as Rene puts it: "There is no word for good-bye in
Anishinaabemowin. We say, 'Minawa apii.' It means to continue our
visit into the times to come. It means to keep our story in the process
till we meet again. We leave each other with a vision. There is a mutual
trust of coming together again, and in the stories we'll be telling."

Miigwetch.

Kim Anderson
March 2019

Notes

1   Liza Mosher, "We Have to go Back to our Original Teachings," in *In the Words of Elders: Aboriginal Cultures in Transition*, ed. Peter Kulchyski, Don McCaskill, and David Newhouse (Toronto: University of Toronto Press, 1999), 141–165.

2   Ibid., 157.

3   Paul Driben, *Aroland is our Home: An Incomplete Victory in Applied Anthropology* (New York: AMS Press, 1986), 23–25.

4   Ibid., 38.

5   Ibid., 34–35.

6   https://en.wikipedia.org/wiki/Greenstone,_Ontario.

7   Ibid.

8   Driben, 33–36.

9   Mark Kuhlberg, "'Nothing it seems can be done about it': Charlie Cox, Indian Affairs, Timber Policy, and the Long Lac Reserve, 1924–40," *Canadian Historical Review* 84, no. 1 (March 2003): 1–17.

10 Ibid.

11 Edward J. Hedican, "On the Rail-Line in Northwestern Ontario: Non-Reserve Housing and Community Change," *Canadian Journal of Native Studies* 10 (1990): 15–32.

12 Mosher, "We Have to go Back to our Original Teachings," 159.

13 Truth and Reconciliation Commission of Canada, *A Knock at the Door: The Essential History of Residential Schools from the Truth and Reconciliation Commission of Canada* (Winnipeg: University of Manitoba Press, 2015), 6.

14 Truth and Reconciliation Commission of Canada, *Honouring the Truth, Reconciling the Future: Summary of the Final Report of the Truth and Reconciliation Commission of Canada* (Ottawa: Truth and Reconciliation Commission of Canada, 2015), 60, 61.

15 Ibid., 63, 69.

16 Ibid., 53–55.

17 John S. Milloy, *A National Crime: The Canadian Government and the Residential School System, 1879 to 1986* (Winnipeg: University of Manitoba Press, 2017).

18 See the Bibliography in Truth and Reconciliation Commission of Canada, *Honouring the Truth, Reconciling the Future*, 408–39.

19 Mosher, "We Have to go Back to our Original Teachings."

20 Ibid.

21 Krista Maxwell, "Making History Heal: Settler-Colonialism and Urban Indigenous Healing in Ontario, 1970s–2010" (PhD diss., Dala Lana School of Public Health, University of Toronto, 2011).

22 http://www.cbc.ca/archives/entry/phil-fontaines-shocking-testimony-of-sexual-abuse.

23 Mosher, "We Have to go Back to our Original Teachings."

24 Ibid.

25 Ibid.

Glossary

adisokan	hero of the story
Adisokewinini	storyteller
Agwanaamon	draw a deep breath
ajijaakons	young crane
akiing	on earth
akikodjiwan	whirlpool
akina	everybody
andjiidana	on purpose
andjishiwebis	change of behaviour
angodjiishan	go away from here
anikanotawing	interpret
anishinaabe	nation from whence lowered
anishinaabeg	(pl.) nation from whence lowered
anishinaabekwe	anishinaabe woman
anishinaabemowin	anishinaabe language
anjiidana	on purpose
anokiitaazo	self-employed
anokiiwin	work
apii	when
apitchi	very much
asawa-shoniia	gold
asemaa	tobacco
ashi	put a person in a certain place
ayaa	being
babiichii	take moccasins off
bebapinisidj	jester

bego	do not
begosha	do not do it
biidaaban	dawn
biiwideg	visitors
bimaadiziwin	life
bingisige	to repel mosquitos with smoke
biwide	visitor
bizaan	be quiet
bizindan	listen
boozho	greeting
'chi	big
chibaie	ghost
chibegamig	grave lodge
debis	to have enough
debisiwin	sufficiency
debwe	tell the truth
dodem	clan
eshinikasi'ian	my name
eshpadinaa	high hill
gagiichii	take off your moccasins
gahmig	lodge
gamadjiinig	take you away
gamiing	lake
gaye	too
gete	old
gichi	great
ginebigoog	snakes
ginebigoons	young snake
giniw	golden eagle
ginwensh	long time
gipi	when
gishe	gracious
gishig	sky
gitchi-aya'aa	elder
gitodem	did you do it?

giwashkwebi	drunk
godjiewisiwin	trial
gondose	walk from
gwaiakoshka	go the right way
gwaiakotam	heard right
imaa	over there
indawendamon	related
indebwe	I tell the truth
indizhinikaaz	my name
ininashawaganak	messengers
inini	man
injichaag	my soul
ishinikasowin	name
ishkode	fire
izhaa	go
jiibik	root
kisha	warm
kissina	cold
kokomissiw	grandmother's
kotagitowin	suffering
maada'oki	share
maadjaa	go
makizinan	shoes
manaadendamowin	respect
Manidoo	God
manidowiwin	spirituality
manitowadis	wealth of spirit
mashkiki	medicine
megwan	feather
memegwessi	little people
migadiing	war
migisiwiganj	eagle claw
miigwetch	thank you
miigwetchi'wendan	grateful
miiwe	give

mikwam	ice
minawa	again
minawako	repeat
mindamokemeshi	monkey
minidimoie	old woman
minidmoieg	old women
mino	good
minobimadisiwin	good life
mishinawew	sharing
mishomisak	grandfather's ancestors
mishoomis	grandfather
mizai	ling fish
modishiwe	go visit
n'zigos	my aunt
naagidisowin	vision
nagaji	skilled
nagamo	sing
neegamowin	song
nenabozho	trickster
neta	talented
nibaan	go to sleep
nidjaaniss	my child
niin	I
niitaga	quiet evening
nindj	hand
nisayneh	my elder brother
nookomis	grandmother
nookomisak	grandmothers
odapinan	you take; you pick up
odena	town
odishinikasowin	his or her name
ogima	chief
ogimakan	designated chief
ogiminan	our mother
ogoki	dive

okomissaag	their grandmothers
omaa	here
ombigidj	raised
oongona	spring water
opwaagan	pipe
ozhaa'washkozi	green
pipigwan	flute
pipigwe	flute language
pipigwew	speak pipigwan language
saagate	sunrise
sainebas	ribbon
sha	go
shaamashkiin	you crouch; you duck
shiwis	merit
songend	strengthen
waabiganoojiinhs	mouse
wabos	rabbit
waabamaken	look at
wegonesh	what?
weshkad	long ago
wiika	ever